Three-Minute Bible Stories Using Activities

by Karen L. Spencer

illustrated by Becky Radtke

3 minutes

Cover by Dan Grossmann

ISBN No. 0-86653-773-2

Standardized Subject Code TA ac

Printing No. 987

Shining Star
A Division of Frank Schaffer Publications, Inc.
23740 Hawthorne Boulevard, Torrance, CA 90505-5927

Unless otherwise indicated, the New International Version of the Bible was used in preparing the activities in this book.

DEDICATION

With love and thanks to my precious children–Josh, Heidi, Shannon, and Eva–for your support and encouragement.

TABLE OF CONTENTS

Holy
Bible

INTRODUCTION

Three-Minute Bible Stories Using Activities was designed for busy teachers. If you have short periods of time when you want to do a quick and meaningful lesson, this book is exactly what you have been looking for.

Both Old and New Testament stories include: Adam and Eve, Cain and Abel, Noah, Moses, Samson and Delilah, David and Goliath, Daniel, Jonah, and over a dozen stories about the life of Jesus. Each story can be told in three minutes. If time allows, it is recommended that children hear the Bible passage read as well as the story included in this book. Scripture references for additional study and memory work are included for your convenience.

Activities include crafts, original songs, games, recipes, action plays, jump rope rhymes, a choral reading, creative writing ideas, a bulletin board, and an Advent calendar. Each activity was especially designed to reinforce details of the story and give children opportunities to display Christian values.

Four fun-filled games to review all the stories are found at the back of the book. An award certificate is also included on page 96.

3 minutes

GOD'S CREATION

Based on Genesis 1:1-2:7

In the beginning there was nothing, nothing but God. There was no sound, no smell, no taste, no touch. No bright yellow sun or puffy white clouds, no big round moon or twinkling stars to make a wish on. There was no land to walk on and no water to swim in. There was nothing, nothing but God.

Then through the emptiness and the silence rang out God's almighty voice, "Let there be light." The darkness was separated from the light, and on the first day, morning and night were created.

On the second day God said, "Let there be an expanse between the waters to separate them," and He created the sky.

On the third day God created dry ground. He called it "land," and He called the waters "seas." Then He said, "Let the land produce vegetation." Suddenly there was soft green grass to lie in and pretty fresh daisies to pick. The trees were heavy with sweet, yummy fruit and vines hung full of grapes. God saw that it was good.

He created the sun to shine and the moon to smile and the stars to twinkle on the fourth day.

On the fifth day God said, "Let the water be filled with living things, and let birds fly in the sky." The air was filled with the sounds of birds singing morning songs and fish jumping high in splashing water. God saw that His creation was good.

He made horses running wild and cattle chewing hay. Squirrels scampered up trees, while lions slept in the sun. That was the sixth day. Then God said, "Let us make man in our image." From the soil He molded a man and breathed into him the breath of life. Man became a living soul.

Oh, what a beautiful world it was that God had made! On day seven He rested from all His work. He blessed the seventh day and made it holy.

SHADOW BOX

Materials:

Shoe box
Blue construction paper
Markers or crayons
Patterns (pages 7-8)
String
Scissors
Tape or glue
Greenery, soil, and pebbles (optional)

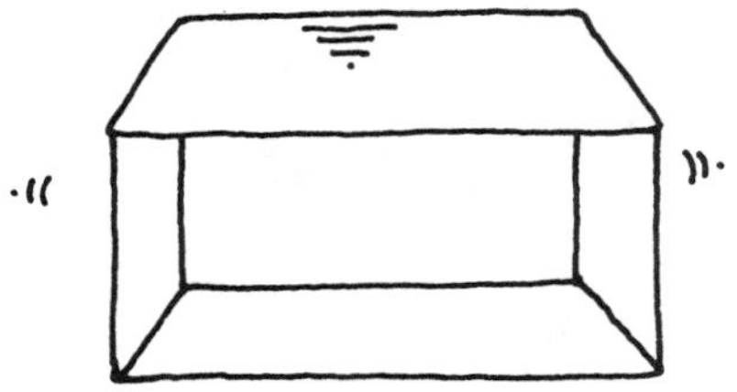

Directions:

Use a shoe box to create the world. Line the box with blue construction paper. Copy the patterns on pages 7 and 8. Color and cut them out. Place the cutouts in the shoe box in the order in which God created them. Hang the sun, moon, and clouds with stars and birds from the top of the shoe box with strings. Real greenery, soil, and pebbles may be added for a special look. Place the man and woman in the front.

Adam
Eve
pebbles, soil, greenery

Fold

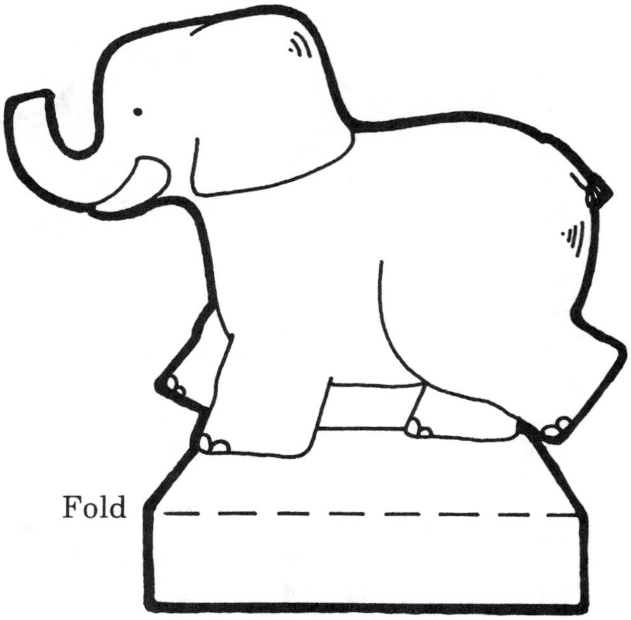

Fold

Tab

Fold

Fold

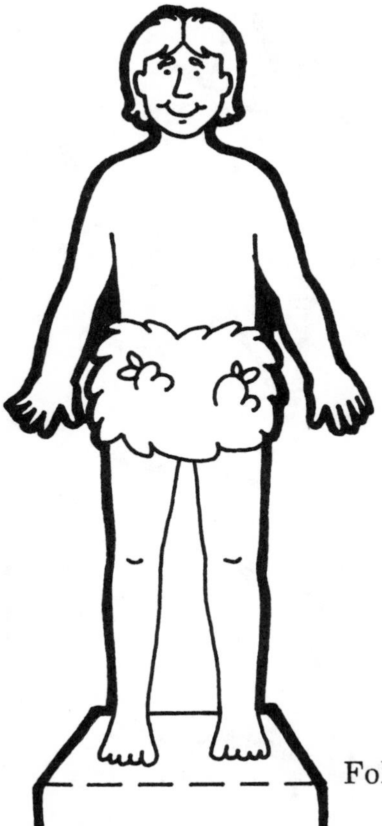

Fold

Fold

Fold

Fold

Fold

ADAM AND EVE

Based on Genesis 2:15-3:24

God created man on the sixth day. God called him Adam. Adam began to name the animals God had created. He noticed that each animal had a partner, but he had none. So, God made him a helpmate.

He caused Adam to sleep and took a rib from Adam's body. God formed a woman from that rib. He brought her to Adam, and she became his wife. Adam called her Eve.

God made a beautiful garden for the man and woman to live in. It was full of delicious food to eat. God wanted Adam to take care of the garden. "Adam, you and Eve are free to eat from any tree in the garden," God said, "but you must not eat from the Tree of the Knowledge of Good and Evil. If you eat of that tree you will die."

One day while Eve was walking peacefully through the garden, someone spoke to her. It was a serpent. "Eve, did God really say you should not eat from any tree in the garden?" asked the serpent.

"Oh no," answered Eve, "God told us that all the trees of the garden are for us to eat from . . . except for that one right there." Eve pointed to a tree in the middle of the garden. "If we touch it, we will die."

The serpent came closer to Eve. "You shall certainly not die," it said, "but if you eat of it you will be like God, knowing good and evil."

Eve was tempted as she looked at the inviting fruit. She thought how wonderful it might be to become wise like God. She reached out, took the fruit, and tasted it. Then Eve told Adam what the serpent had said and convinced him to also eat the forbidden fruit.

As soon as Adam and Eve tasted the fruit, they knew they had sinned. They were ashamed and afraid.

That evening God called, "Where are you, Adam?"

Adam was hiding behind a bush. He slowly peeked out and answered with fear, "I heard You in the Garden and I was afraid, so I hid."

"Have you eaten from the tree that I commanded you not to eat?" God asked.

Adam pointed to where Eve was hiding and blamed her. "The woman You put here with me gave me some fruit and I ate it."

Eve came quickly forward, "It wasn't my fault," she said. "It was that serpent. He lied to me and convinced me that I should eat the fruit."

God said to the serpent, "You will crawl on your belly and eat dust all the days of your life!"

Because of their sin, Adam and Eve were banished from the beautiful garden. From that day on, their lives would be filled with hard work and pain.

What a sad day it was! But God loved Adam and Eve, and although they had to be punished, He promised to someday send a Savior to forgive their sins.

STICK PUPPETS

Materials:

Markers or crayons
Patterns (from this page)
Glue
Scissors
Craft sticks

Crayons
glue

God

Directions:

Color and cut out the figures on this page, and glue them to craft sticks. Use the puppets to show what happened in the Garden of Eden.

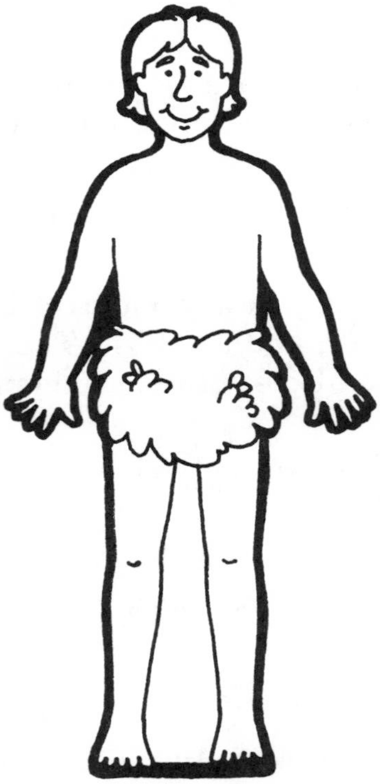

Adam

Eve

Forbidden tree

Serpent

God

God

CAIN AND ABEL

Based on Genesis 4

God blessed Adam and Eve with two sons. One was named Cain, the other was named Abel. Cain worked in the fields to grow food for his family. Abel took care of flocks of sheep.

Adam and Eve and their two sons often brought offerings to the Lord. One day Abel gave an offering to God. Abel loved God, so he was especially careful to offer one of the best sheep in his flock. Cain also gave an offering, but Cain did not choose the best of his crop to bring to God.

God was happy with Abel's offering but not with Cain's. He knew that Cain did not bring the offering with love in his heart. Cain became angry.

The Lord said to Cain, "Why are you angry? Why do you look sad? If you do not do what is right, more sin will come into your life." God was right. More sin *did* come into Cain's life.

Cain was jealous of Abel and his hatred grew strong. One day Cain said to Abel, "Let's go out to the field." While they were there, Cain attacked Abel and killed him.

God's angry voice called out to Cain, "Where is your brother Abel?"

"How should I know?" snapped guilty Cain, "Am I always supposed to watch out for my brother?"

"What have you done?" the Lord asked. "Listen! Your brother's blood cried out to me from the ground. Cain, now you are under a curse. You must leave this place and find somewhere else to live."

Cain begged God not to make him leave. "I will not be able to be near You anymore, and I will not ever be able to find a place to live. Whoever sees me will kill me!"

The Lord said to him, "No one will kill you, Cain, for I will put a mark on you so that others will know who you are."

God knew how sad Adam and Eve were to have both of their sons gone. He blessed them with another son and they called him Seth.

FAMILY TREE

The Bible tells about the family God gave Adam and Eve. Tell about the family God gave you by making this family tree.

Materials:

Small branch
Markers or crayons
Can
Plastic clay or rocks
Drawing paper
Scissors
String
Tape

crayons

Directions:

Stick the branch into a can filled with clay or rocks. Have the child draw pictures of all the people in his family and cut them out. Tape a piece of string to each drawing. Tie it to the family tree.

me
dad
mom
Lisa

NOAH'S ARK

Based on Genesis 6:1-9:17

God looked down upon the earth and was very angry. He saw evil people doing wicked things. These people didn't love God or care about Him. So God decided to destroy everyone . . . everyone but Noah and his family.

God said to Noah, "I am sad that all the people on earth have become so wicked. They are not sorry for their sins. I will wipe everything from the face of the earth–people, animals, creatures that move along the ground, and birds of the air. For I am sorry I made them."

God told Noah that He was going to send a flood that would destroy the whole world. Noah was to follow instructions and build a boat large enough to hold all his family, two of every animal, and food enough for all of them.

Each day Noah and his family hammered away, putting the boat together. The neighbors laughed and teased as they watched Noah working hard. But Noah and his family didn't listen. Imagine what the neighbors thought as they saw two of each kind of animal being loaded onto the enormous boat!

Finally everything was completed. The animals were on the ark, Noah's family was on the ark, and there was enough food for all of them. The rain began to fall as God closed the door on the huge boat.

The neighbors' laughter turned to fear as they watched the rain continue to fall. It rained and rained and rained. The water in the lakes and streams began overflowing. For forty days and nights the water crept up on the mountains until there was no dry land left. The world and all the people on it were destroyed. But Noah and his family were safe and dry inside the boat. They floated in the water for 150 days. Then God sent a wind, and the waters began to go down.

Noah sent a raven out of the ark but it did not return. Then he sent out a dove. The dove came back, for it could find no dry place to land. Again, Noah sent out the dove. This time it came back with a fresh olive leaf in its beak. Noah knew the water was going down.

At last God told Noah to come out of the ark with his family and animals. The first thing Noah did was build an altar and bring an offering to thank the Lord.

God promised Noah, "Never again will I destroy the earth with a flood." God put a beautiful rainbow in the sky as a sign of His promise.

ANIMAL MATCHING GAME

Materials:

Glue
Poster board
Scissors

Directions:

Make two copies of this page and page 15. Glue on poster board and cut out the cards. Play the game as you would play "Go Fish." Shuffle the cards. Pass out five cards to each player. The players try to make pairs. A player asks the person on his right, "Do you have an elephant (or a card that will allow him to make a pair)?" If the person has an elephant, he gives it to the player, and the player gets another turn. If the person does not have an elephant, he says, "Go ask Noah." The player draws a card from the pile. If the card is an elephant, the player gets another turn. If the card is not an elephant, the person on the right takes his turn. Pairs should be put facedown on the table. The player with the most pairs at the end of the game wins.

Lion
Monkey
Bear
Giraffe
Zebra
Lamb

Bird
Tiger
Butterfly
Hippopotamus
Kangaroo
Elephant
Rhinoceros
Camel
Rabbit

NOAH'S ARK

Karen L. Spencer

F F G G7
"No - ah, build an ark," God said. "Build it big and wide.
"Ga - ther up My an - i - mals, two of ev - 'ry kind, and
C7 C7 C7 F
I will send a flood to earth, but you'll be safe in - side." And the rain went
when the flood is o - ver I will send a spe - cial sign."
F F G G G7
drip drip drip, and the rain went drop drop drop, and the rain went
C C7 C7 1 F
drip drip drop drop drip drip drop drop. Will it ev - er stop?
2 F F F G
stop? At last the rain was o - ver and the earth be - gan to
G7 C C C7
dry. O - ver - head a rain - bow, God's pro - mise in the
F F F G
sky; and it did - n't drip drip drip, and it did - n't drop drop
G7 C C7
drop, and it did - n't drip drip drop drop drip drip drop drop. Shh - hh - hh - hh
C7 F
Lis - ten. The rain has stopped.

MOSES, A VERY SPECIAL CHILD

Based on Exodus 1:1-2:10

God had chosen the Israelites to be His special people. One day the Savior, Jesus, would be born from them. God looked after His chosen people and cared for them.

Because of a great famine, Israelites had come to the land of Egypt. They continued to live there, and God blessed them with many children.

Egypt's ruler was called Pharaoh. He wanted his country to be very powerful. He began to worry that there were too many Israelites.

Pharaoh decided to get rid of some of God's people. He put slave masters over them. He made them build cities. He thought that if he made them work very hard, some Israelites would die and fewer babies would be born. But the harder the Israelites worked, the stronger they became.

This worried Pharaoh even more. "I want all the baby Israelite boys thrown into the river and drowned, " he ordered. What a sad time! Crying was heard all over Egypt as the Israelites prayed to God.

A baby boy was born to an Israelite father and mother. They could not bear to have their child killed, so they hid him from the soldiers. After three months the mother made a basket and covered it with pitch so it would float. She gently laid her baby in the basket, covered him, and placed the basket in the tall grasses at the edge of the river. The baby's sister, Miriam, watched from a distance to see what would happen.

When Pharaoh's daughter came to the water to take a bath, she noticed the basket floating in the reeds. She pulled back the covers and, to her surprise, saw a baby's eyes looking at her. The baby began to cry. The princess gently lifted him from the basket. "This is one of the Israelite babies," she said, "I will take him and keep him safe."

Miriam was watching closely. She came toward Pharaoh's daughter and asked, "Shall I get a woman of Israel to take care of the baby for you?" The princess agreed and Miriam quickly went to get her mother.

How happy the baby's mother was to know her son was safe! She took her baby home and cared for him until he grew older. Then she took him to Pharaoh's daughter. The baby became the princess' son, and she named him Moses.

"GOD'S GARDEN OF LOVE" BULLETIN BOARD

Moses was a very special baby. God had chosen him to one day lead the people of Israel. Like Moses, each one of us is also special in God's eyes. Make a bulletin board about "God's Garden of Love."

Materials:

Light brown craft or wrapping paper
Construction paper: red, blue, purple, white, yellow, green
Patterns (page 19)
Green pipe cleaners
Scissors
Glue
Crayons
Stapler (optional)

Directions:

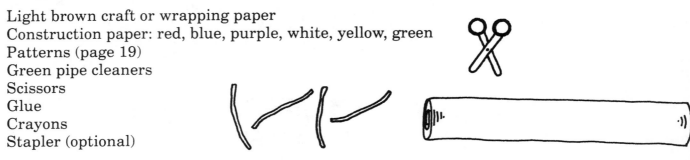

Trace each child's hand on a piece of construction paper and cut it out. (Some children's fingers may be spread out, others may be held closely together to make different looking flowers. Right or left hands may be traced.)

To make some flowers different, fold the thumb and baby finger cutouts inward and glue in place.

Glue or staple handprints to a bulletin board which you have covered with brown paper.

Use green construction paper or green pipe cleaners to make flower stems (see patterns on page 19). Glue the stems under the flowers. Have the children write their names by flowers.

Point out to the children that each flower is different yet very special, just like each of us is special to God.

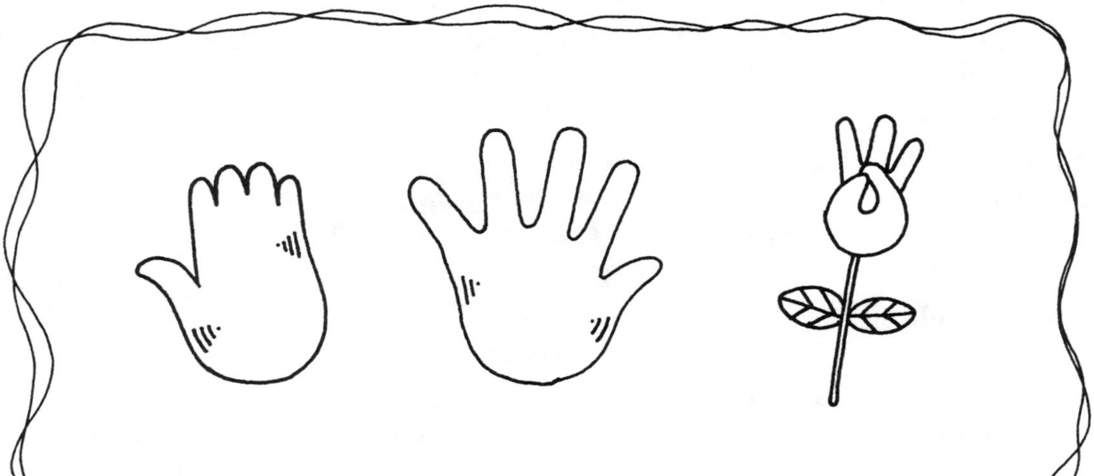

Stem Pattern

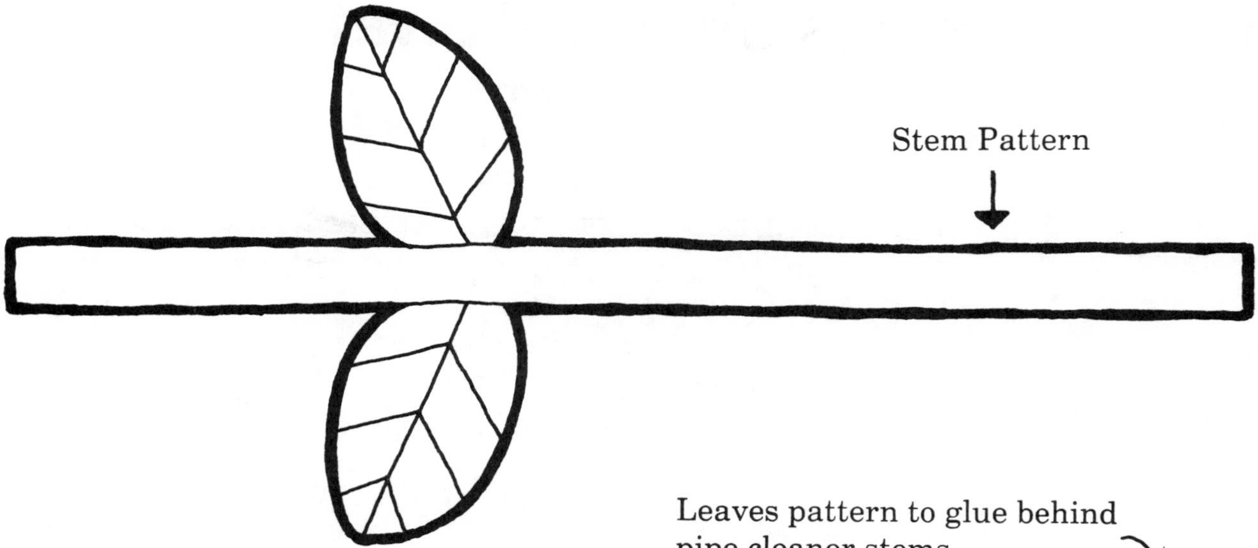

Leaves pattern to glue behind pipe cleaner stems.

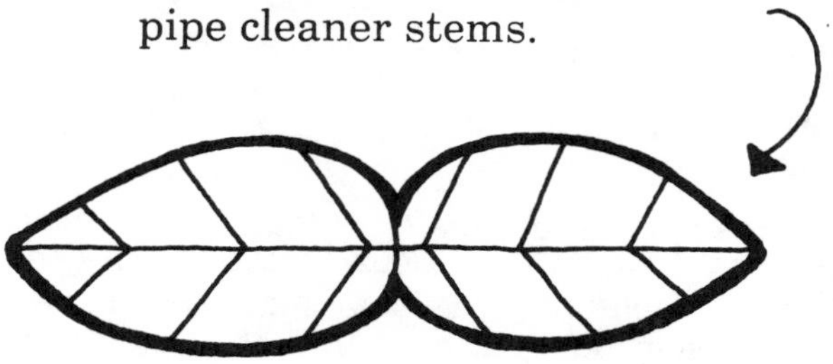

Fold and glue.

God's Garden of Love
Mary
John
Bill
Tammy

God's Garden of Love

Karen L. Spencer

C C C
1. God takes a ti - ny seed and then He plants it with care. He
2. I am a tu - lip and I am a rose.
3. My co - lor is pur - ple; my pet - als are blue.
4. When you're feel - ing down, you're not as good as the rest. When you
G7 G7 C
o - pens up His heart and gives, each one a share. He makes them grow big - ger and He
I am a dai - sy 'cuz that's how it goes. I am a vio - let as
I am kind of crook - ed 'cuz that's how I grew. All of us are diff - 'rent; that's
think that be - ing some-thing else is prob - ab - ly best. Think what a drag the
C7 F G G7 C
lets them grow tall. He cares for them e - qual - ly, one and all.
shy as can be. But that's o - kay 'cuz God made me.
plain to see. 'Cuz God made us so spe - cial - ly.
world would be if flow - ers looked a - like ex - act - ly.
Chorus
C C C
Oh we're all spe - cial flow - ers in God's gar - den of love. We're
(Last time)
Do do do do do do do do do do do do do do. do
G G7 C
all spe - cial flow - ers in God's gar - den of love.
do do do do do do do do do do do.

THE PLAGUES

Based on Exodus 7:14-12:41

Moses and his brother, Aaron, were chosen by God to lead the Israelites out of Egypt and into the Promised Land. But the ruler of Egypt was stubborn. He wanted the Israelites to stay in Egypt and be his slaves.

"Let my people go!" demanded Moses to Pharaoh. "The Lord, my God, will punish you and your people if you do not let the Israelites leave Egypt."

The Pharaoh shook his head, "No!"

God told Aaron to stretch out his hand over the waters of Egypt–all the streams, canals, ponds, and lakes. When Moses and Aaron did as the Lord had commanded, the waters turned to blood! All the fish died and the Egyptians could not drink.

But Pharaoh did not love God and did not want to obey Him. "I will not let these people of Israel go. I will make them work harder. We will beat them until they die!" he said.

God told Aaron to stretch out his rod over the rivers and ponds. This time frogs came up and covered the land. They hopped around in houses and on people. Thousands and thousands of frogs were leaping through the kingdom. At last Pharaoh screamed, "I promise to let the people go if only your God will take away the frogs!" But when God took away the frogs, Pharaoh did not keep his promise.

God sent another plague to Egypt. Tiny, stinging bugs called gnats crawled from the dust onto the animals and people, biting them until the people cried to Pharaoh to let the Israelites go. Again, Pharaoh promised to let the people go if the gnats were taken away. But again, he broke his promise.

The next time, the Lord sent a plague of flies that swarmed through the Egyptian palace. Then He sent a terrible disease that killed all the cattle that belonged to the Egyptians. Pharaoh still refused to let God's people go.

The Lord said to Moses, "Toss handfuls of soot into the air." Moses did, and horrible, painful sores broke out on all the Egyptian people and their animals.

A hailstorm, locusts, and a plague of darkness also came on the land. But Pharaoh still refused to let the people of Israel go.

The Lord sent one more plague. All the firstborn male children in Egypt died, but not one of the Israelites was harmed. What a sad morning when the Egyptians awoke. Crying was heard all across the land. Pharaoh's oldest son lay dead. "Leave," wailed Pharaoh. "Take these Israelites from my sight."

The Israelites left the land of Egypt. Hundreds of thousands of God's people walked together, following Moses and Aaron. Israelites had been in Egypt for 430 years. Now God was keeping His promise, leading His people to the Promised Land.

PLAGUE BINGO

Materials:

Scissors
Glue

Directions:

Make several copies of the plague pictures on page 23 and the bingo card below. Cut out the pictures and glue them on the bingo cards in different orders. (Each card should be different.) Keep one set of plague pictures separate. Put them in a container for use when calling out the plagues.

Give each child a bingo card and some buttons, small crackers, or cereal for markers. Draw a plague picture and call it out for the group. Each child puts a marker on that picture. When a child gets three markers in a row–across, down, or diagonally–have him stand up and say, "Let my people go!"

"PLAGUE BINGO" PATTERNS

Blood

Frogs

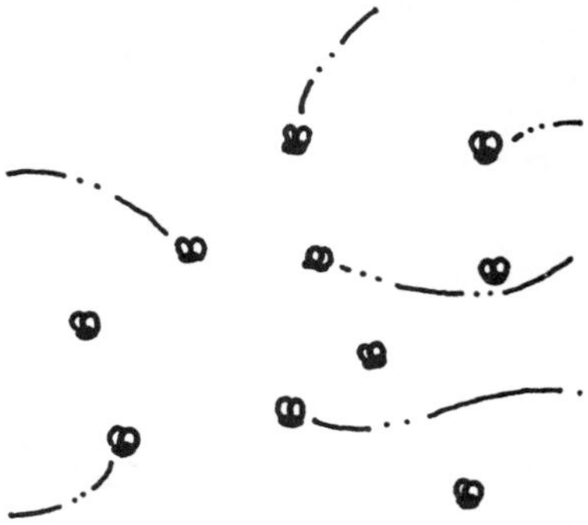

Flies

Gnats

Disease on Animals

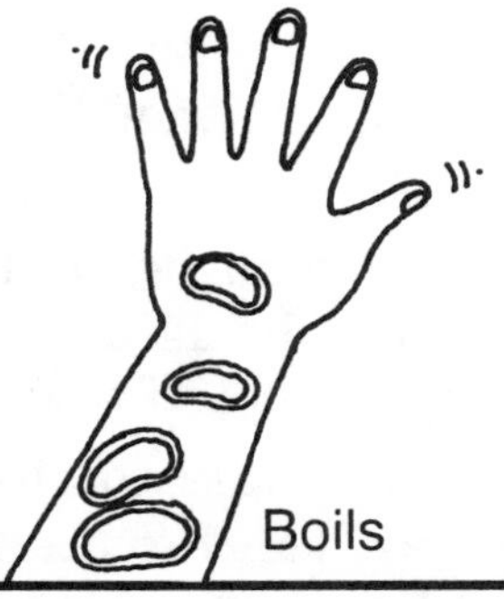

Boils

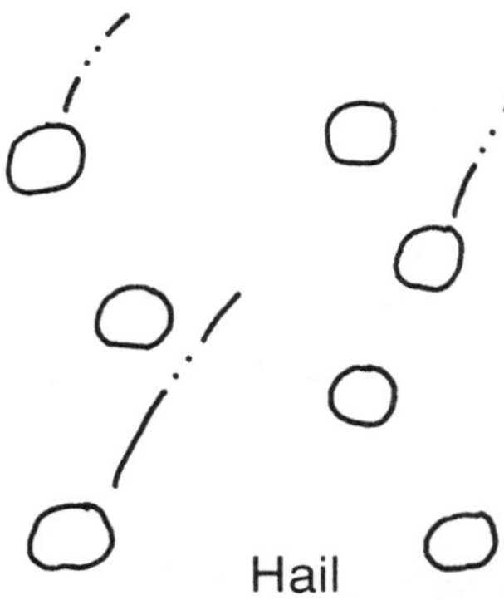

Hail

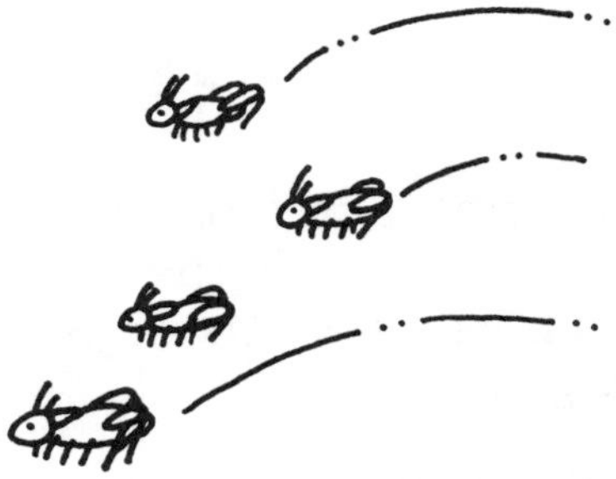

Locusts

Darkness

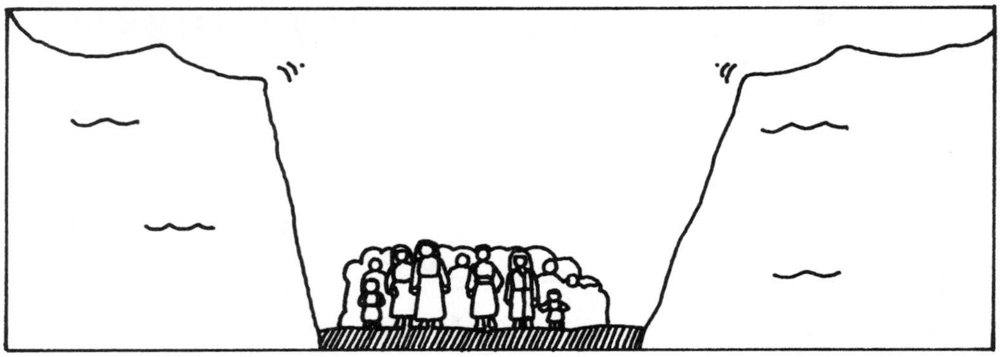

CROSSING THE RED SEA

Based on Exodus 13:17-14:31

When Pharaoh finally agreed to let them go, the Israelites packed a few belongings and hurried away. Through the desert they walked, in search of the free land God had promised them. By day the Lord went ahead of them in a pillar of cloud and by night in a pillar of fire. Neither the pillar of cloud nor the pillar of fire left its place in front of the people.

Pharaoh soon realized that he should not have let Moses and Aaron lead their people away. With all the Israelites gone there was no one to work for him. He gathered his army and marched off to find the Israelites.

God led His people to the edge of the Red Sea to camp for the night. When the Israelites saw the Egyptian soldiers coming after them they cried out, "Why did you bring us out of Egypt, Moses? It would have been better for us to serve Pharaoh than to die in the desert."

Moses called to his people, "Do not be afraid. The Lord will fight for you; just be still and believe."

The Lord told Moses, "Raise your staff and stretch out your hand over the sea." When Moses did this, the pillar of cloud moved from the front and stood behind them, coming between the armies of Egypt and Israel. All night the cloud brought darkness to Egypt's side and light to Israel's side.

All that night the Lord drove the sea back with a strong wind, until it became dry land. The waters were divided, and the Israelites walked through the sea on dry ground, with a wall of water on their right and on their left.

The next morning the Egyptians saw how the seas had parted. They drove their chariots after the Israelites. Then the Lord said to Moses, "Stretch out your hand over the sea so that the waters will flow back over the Egyptians and their chariots and horsemen."

Moses stretched out his hand over the sea, and at daybreak the sea went back to its place. The water covered all the chariots and horsemen, the whole army of Pharaoh. Not one of them was left alive. Not one of the Israelites was harmed. The Lord had saved Israel from the hands of the Egyptians.

When the Israelites saw the great power the Lord had shown against the Egyptians, the people feared the Lord and put their trust in Him and in Moses.

UNLEAVENED BREAD AND RED SEA PUNCH

Today many Jewish people still celebrate Passover. The tradition began 3000 years ago when the Hebrews were forced to flee from Egypt. While they were getting ready for their trip, they didn't have enough time to wait for yeast bread to rise. So they quickly baked unleavened bread to take with them.

Make unleavened bread for a snack and serve it with Red Sea punch.

Unleavened Bread

Ingredients:

2 cups whole wheat flour

$^1/_2$ tsp salt

$^1/_2$ to $^3/_4$ cup warm water

whole
wheat
flour

Directions:

1. Blend flour and salt in mixing bowl.
2. Add water until dough is evenly moist and sticks together.
3. Knead on floured surface. At first the dough will be crumbly, but after kneading about 5 minutes it will become smooth.
4. Divide dough in half and roll out on floured surface. Dough should be about $^1/_8$" thick and slightly smaller than the griddle on which it will be cooked.
5. Lightly flour the griddle and place over low heat.
6. Place the dough on the griddle and cook 15-18 minutes on each side. Bread is done when the outside is crisp but the inside is still slightly soft.

Red Sea Punch

Ingredients:

2 quarts cranberry juice cocktail, chilled

1 can (6 oz) frozen pink lemonade concentrate, thawed

1 quart sparkling water, chilled

pink
lemonade

Directions:

Mix cranberry juice cocktail and lemonade concentrate in a large punch bowl. Just before serving, stir in sparkling water.

THE TEN COMMANDMENTS

Based on Exodus 19:1-20; 24:1-18; 31:18; 32:1-33; 34:1-6, 28-33

The Israelites were camped at the foot of Mt. Sinai. Three months had passed since the Lord had led them out of Egypt.

The Lord spoke to Moses from the top of the mountain, "I saved the Israelites from the Egyptians, and I carried them safely to this spot. If they obey all that I say, then they will be My own special people."

After the Israelites agreed, God came and spoke to them. There was thunder and lightning. A very loud trumpet blast was heard, and a thick cloud covered the mountain. Everyone in the camp trembled with fear as they stood at the foot of the mountain.

God spoke to the people of Israel about ten special laws called the Ten Commandments that they were to obey. The first three laws told the people how they were supposed to honor and obey God. They were not to worship any other god or make an idol and pray to it. They were to treat God's name with respect. They were to remember the seventh day and keep it holy. God also told them they were to love and respect their parents. In the next five commandments God told the people how to treat each other.

The people of Israel promised to obey God's laws.

God called Moses to the top of the mountain. Moses stayed for forty days. God told him all the rules the Israelites were to obey. God wrote the Commandments on two tablets of stone. He gave them to Moses to carry back to his people.

While Moses was speaking with God, the Israelites grew tired of waiting for their leader to return. "What if Moses never returns?" they complained. "Who will take care of us then?" They told Aaron, Moses' brother, to make them a god that would lead them to the Promised Land of Canaan.

Not wanting to hear the people complain anymore, Aaron told them to take off all their gold jewelry and bring it to the fire. He put the gold into a pot, melted it down, and formed the melted gold into the shape of a calf.

The people of Israel prayed to the calf as if it were the Lord. Then they began to celebrate by getting drunk and dancing around wildly. They worshiped and sacrificed to the calf idol.

When Moses arrived back at the camp, he saw his people dancing and praying to the calf. His heart burned with anger. He threw down the tablets of stone and shattered them. Moses rushed to the idol formed from gold and flung it into the fire.

Moses ached for his people and their sins against God. He fell on his knees and prayed. "Dear Father, please forgive these people who have committed a great sin." He begged, "Let me be punished for them."

The Lord forgave His people, but He said, "If the Israelites continue to disobey Me, they will bring an awful punishment on themselves."

The people of Israel felt great sorrow for their sins. Once again, they promised to obey God.

CHORAL READING

Based on Psalm 23

God led His people out of Egypt, across the Red Sea, through the desert. He gave them rules to keep them happy. He watched over them and cared for them like a shepherd cares for his sheep.

Copy this choral reading for each child. Have the class read it together.

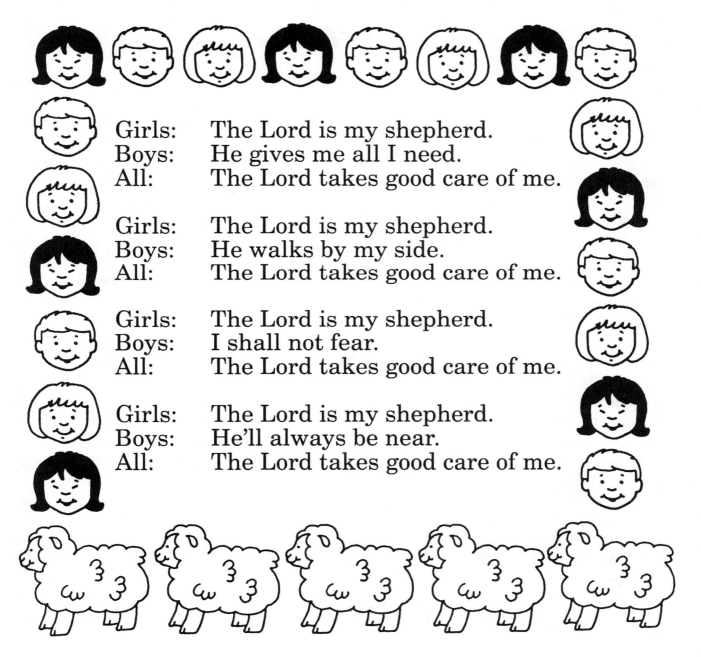

Girls: The Lord is my shepherd.
Boys: He gives me all I need.
All: The Lord takes good care of me.

Girls: The Lord is my shepherd.
Boys: He walks by my side.
All: The Lord takes good care of me.

Girls: The Lord is my shepherd.
Boys: I shall not fear.
All: The Lord takes good care of me.

Girls: The Lord is my shepherd.
Boys: He'll always be near.
All: The Lord takes good care of me.

SAMSON AND DELILAH

Based on Judges 13-16

The Israelites, God's chosen people, again turned away from God. They forgot about all the times God had helped them. They began to worship other gods. The Lord was angry. He wanted His people to stop their evil ways and return to Him. So He allowed the Philistine people to become very powerful and rule over the Israelites.

But God did not turn away from His people. One day the angel of the Lord appeared to a woman of Israel and said, "You are going to have a son. He will begin to free Israel from the Philistines. As a sign that he is to do this special work, his hair must never be cut."

Just as God had promised, the baby was born. His mother named him Samson. As the boy grew, God blessed him and made him very strong. Samson knew that he was special and that God wanted to use his strength to free the Israelites from the Philistines.

One day Samson came upon a lion. God gave him the power to kill the lion, tearing it apart with his bare hands.

The Philistines hated Samson because of his strength. They tried to find a way to destroy him. Samson fell in love with a Philistine woman named Delilah. The rulers of the Philistines came to visit Delilah. They promised to give her silver if she could discover the secret of Samson's great strength.

Delilah loved money, so she agreed to trick Samson. She pretended to care about him very much. She begged him to tell her his secret. Each time Delilah begged Samson, he made up a story about how he got his strength.

Samson began to love Delilah more than God. She continued to beg Samson until he could stand it no longer. "If my head were shaved, my strength would leave me, and I would become as weak as any man," he told her.

Delilah let Samson fall asleep with his head on her lap. She had someone shave his head; then she called the Philistines.

Samson jumped up to fight, but his strength was gone. The Philistines grabbed him and poked out his eyes. They led him off in chains and put him in prison. Slowly, Samson's hair began to grow again.

One day the Philistines had a special celebration in the temple to honor their god, Dagon. The rulers asked that Samson be brought out of prison to entertain them. Samson could hear all the noise of the people celebrating and worshiping their false god. He called out to the Lord, "Please strengthen me once more. Let me, with one blow, get revenge on the Philistines."

He reached out and grabbed two pillars on which the temple stood. Bracing himself against the giant pillars, he pushed with all his might. Down came the temple on the rulers and all the people in it.

ISRAELITES AGAINST PHILISTINES

Red Rover

Play this game of strength. Divide into teams and play a familiar game of Red Rover. Select a captain for each team. As in Red Rover, the teams join arms to make a chain-like wall. Name one team the Samson team and the other the Philistine team.

Have the Samson team shout, "Red Rover, Red Rover, send a Philistine right over." The Philistine team captain chooses a team member to run and try to break through a weak link in the Samson team. If the player breaks through, he may take a member of the Samson team to join his own. If the player doesn't break through, he must join the Samson team. Then it's time for the Philistine team to shout, "Red Rover, Red Rover, send Samson right over." The captain of the Samson team chooses a team member to try to break the Philistine line.

The team that has the most members at the end of the game wins.

Indoor Olympics

Divide the class in two groups, the Israelites and the Philistines, for indoor Olympics. Keep score as each event is played. Encourage the teams to make up cheers to cheer on their players.

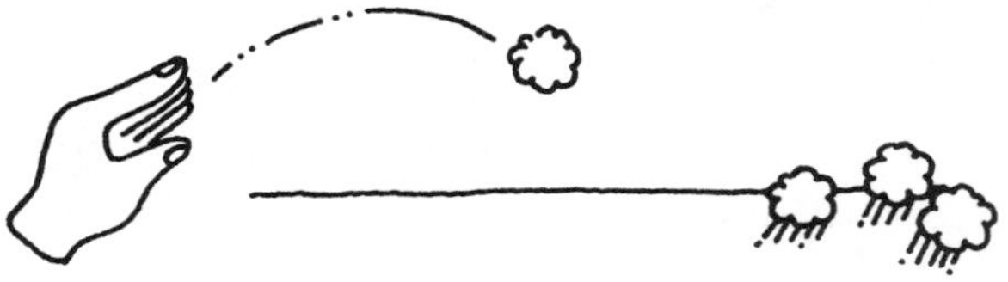

Ball Toss:

See who can throw a cotton ball the farthest.

Plate Toss:

Have a paper plate toss to see who can come closest to the marked target.

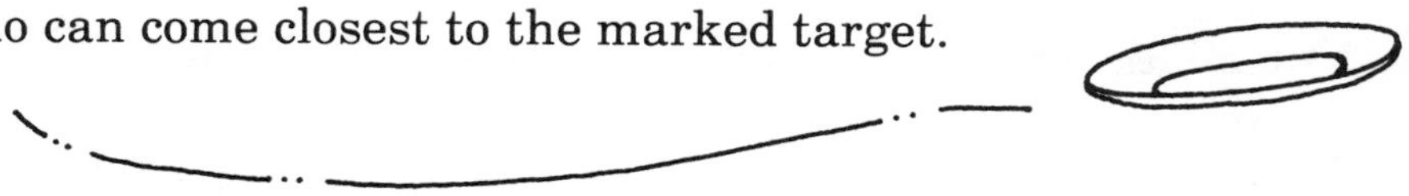

Ping-Pong Hockey:

Cut out a cardboard box for a "playing field." Each player uses a straw to try to blow a Ping-Pong™ ball to the opposite goal.

Balloon Pop:

Have each child blow up a balloon, and then see who can pop his first.

Lid Toss:

Draw a face on a paper plate. Cut out a big circle for the mouth. Attach the plate to a paint stick or ruler. Give each player three plastic milk bottle lids. See how many lids each one can toss through the opening of the mouth.

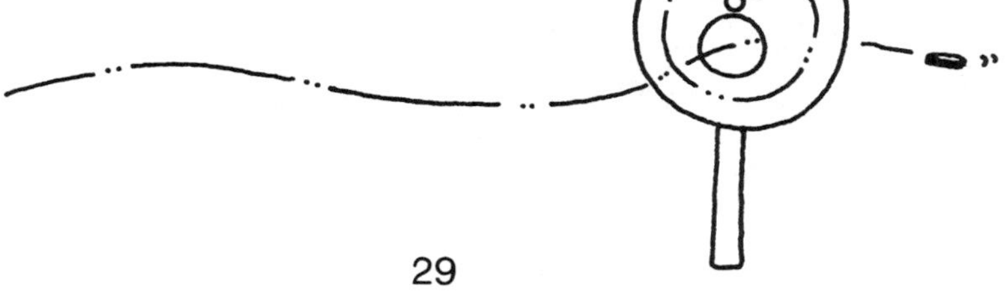

DAVID AND GOLIATH

Based on 1 Samuel 17

As the sun slipped into the mountains, the sounds of David's harp could be heard in the hills of Judea. The shepherd boy played and sang praises to God.

David was the youngest of Jesse's eight sons. One day Jesse sent David with food for his three older brothers, who were with the army of Israelites getting ready to do battle with the Philistines.

As David reached his brothers' camp, he saw the army going out to its battle positions. David quickly found his brothers and began talking with them. Suddenly, a Philistine named Goliath came out from the camp across the valley. He was a giant, almost ten feet tall! He had a bronze helmet on his head and he wore a heavy coat of armor. His spear was made of iron.

Goliath's voice bellowed across the valley, "Why do you come out and line up for battle? Aren't I a Philistine, and aren't you the servants of Saul? Choose a man and have him come down to me. I will fight him. Whoever wins will be the master over the other."

When the Israelite soldiers saw the giant, they ran from him in fear. David asked, "What will be done for the man who kills this Philistine and removes this disgrace from Israel? Who is this man that he should go against the armies of the living God?" David stood tall and announced, "I will fight the giant."

Down toward the valley David marched closer to the Philistine. The young boy didn't carry a sword. Instead he had a slingshot and five smooth rocks in his pouch.

Goliath saw David coming and laughed angrily. "You are only a boy!"

David stood bravely before the Philistine. "You come against me with sword and spear and javelin, but I come against you in the name of the Lord Almighty, the God of the armies of Israel. This day the Lord will hand you over to me."

David reached into his bag and took out a stone as Goliath began running toward him. David circled the sling in the air, then slung the rock and hit the Philistine on the forehead. The giant fell dead on the ground.

David had killed the giant, but the victory was the Lord's.

CARDBOARD ARMOR

Materials:

Three cardboard fruit box dividers
Yarn
Felt strips
Newspapers
Stapler
Tape
Hole punch
Large nail

Directions:

Ask a produce worker at your local market for cardboard fruit box dividers (apple season is a good time to find them). Punch a hole about halfway down each side of the two dividers, and tie a 12" piece of yarn through each hole. Cut two 1" x 9" strips of felt, and staple them to the top of the dividers, joining the two pieces. Be careful that the felt is far enough apart for the "armor" to fit over the child's head. Once the armor is in place, secure by tying the pieces of yarn.

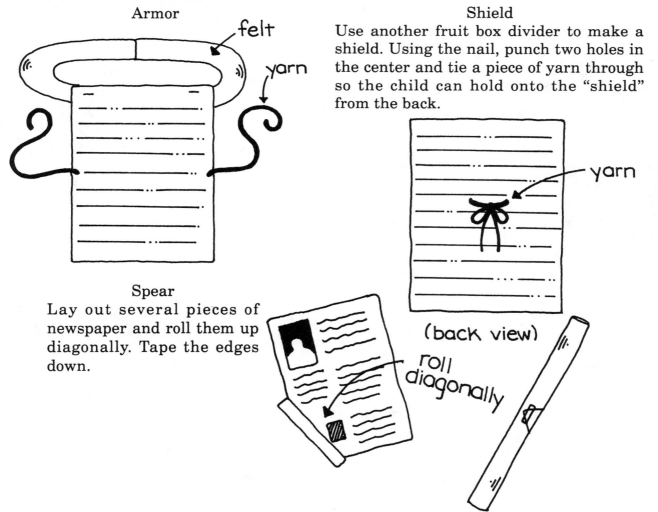

Armor

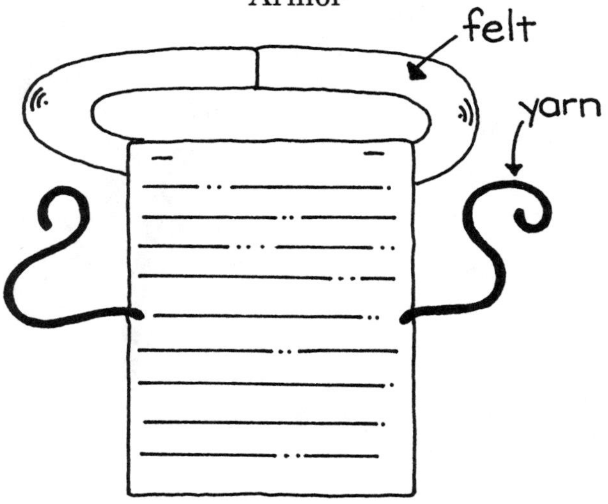
felt
yarn

Shield

Use another fruit box divider to make a shield. Using the nail, punch two holes in the center and tie a piece of yarn through so the child can hold onto the "shield" from the back.

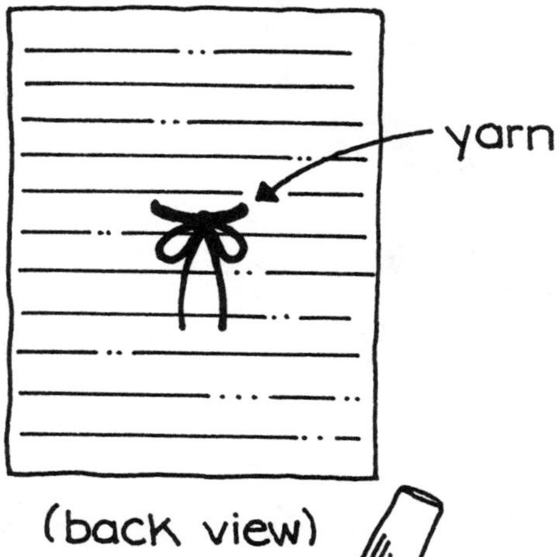
yarn
(back view)

Spear

Lay out several pieces of newspaper and roll them up diagonally. Tape the edges down.

roll
diagonally

DAVID'S HARP

Materials:

Heavy cardboard
Three colored rubber bands
Six brad fasteners
Harp pattern
Scissors

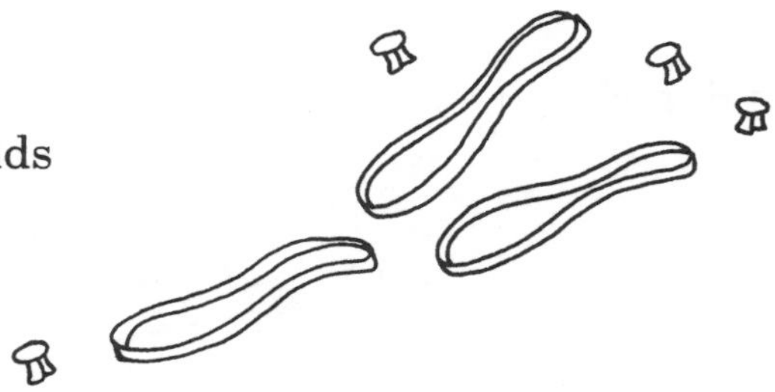

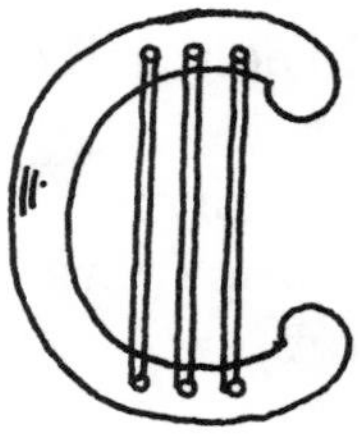

Directions:

Trace the harp below on a heavy piece of cardboard and cut it out. Put the brad fasteners where the Xs are. Hook a rubber band around the brad at the top. Secure the back end of the brad, and hold the rubber band in place while hooking the rubber band on the parallel brad. Do this with all three rubber bands.

When the harp is completed, sing the following words to the tune of "You Are My Sunshine" and strum along.

"You are my strength, Lord, my shield and armor.

You keep me safe from all my foes.

I'll pray to You, God, and sing Your praises.

Please stay close, and comfort me."

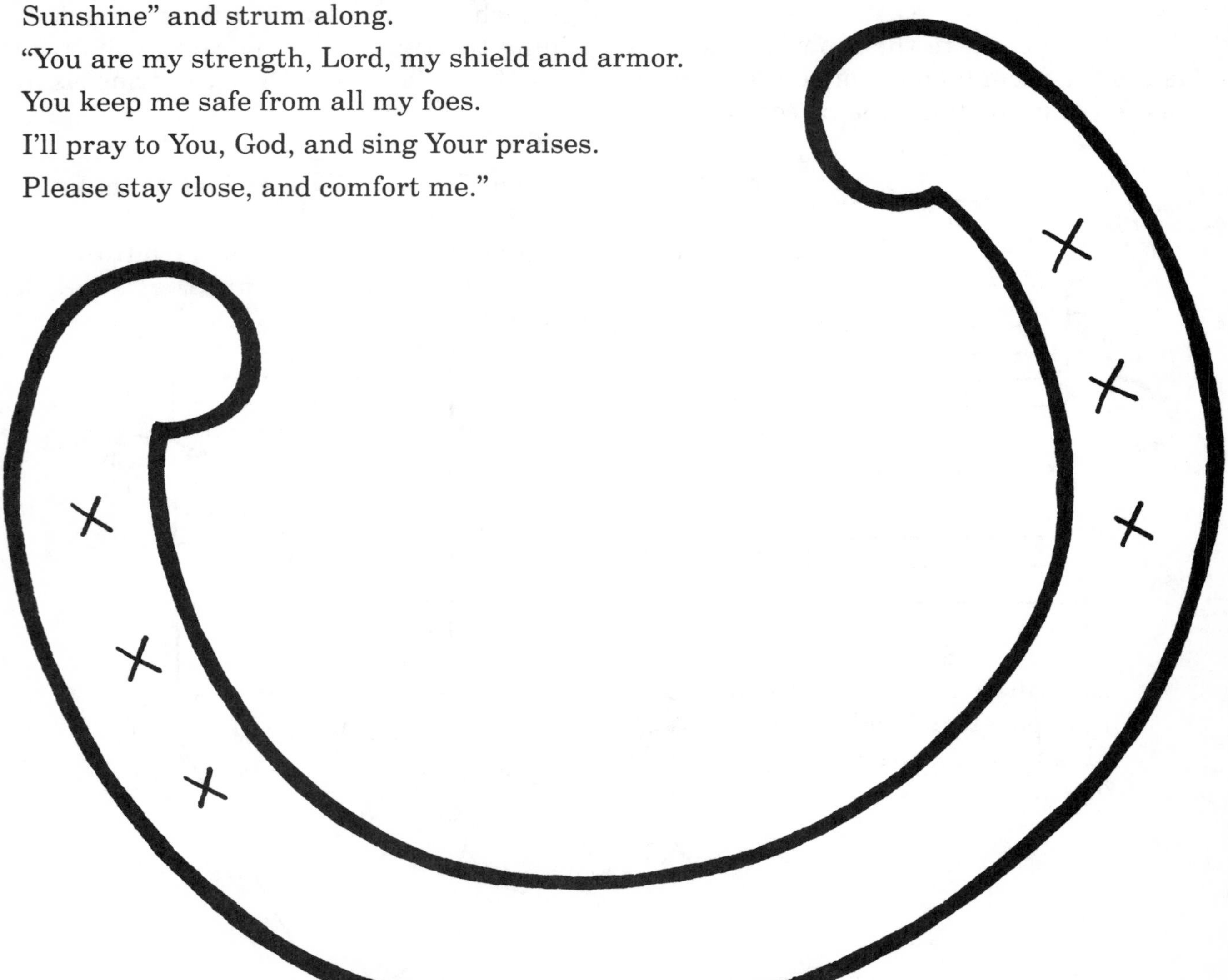

DANIEL IN THE LIONS' DEN

Based on Daniel 6

Once there was a good king named Darius. As every king does, he chose people to help him. One of the helpers King Darius chose was a man named Daniel.

Daniel loved the Lord and often prayed to Him. He thanked God for all the good things He had given him. Daniel was also a hard worker. That pleased the king, and Daniel became very powerful in the country. The other helpers did not like to see how much King Darius liked Daniel. They were jealous, so they began to think of a way to get rid of him.

The evil men watched Daniel to find something that he was doing wrong. But Daniel was very honest and trustworthy, and the men couldn't find anything wrong with him.

One day they saw Daniel in an upstairs window of his house, praying to God. They knew he did that often. That gave the men an idea for an evil plan to get rid of him.

The men went to King Darius and said, "Because you are such a great king, the people in your kingdom should bow down to you and worship you. You should pass a new law that says if anyone prays to a god or another man besides you, he should be thrown into a den of lions." The king thought the idea was a good one and signed the new law.

When Daniel heard about the new law, he was sad. He loved God and would not stop praying to Him, no matter what. The king's helpers waited until Daniel went to his home. They caught him praying to God. They dragged him before the king.

"See, your majesty, your servant Daniel pays no attention to you. He still prays to his God three times a day." King Darius had been tricked.

"Daniel, I am sorry," said the king. "May your God, that you pray to, rescue you from the mouths of the hungry lions." Then the king ordered Daniel to be taken to the den. He was pushed inside and a big stone was rolled over the door so he could not escape.

The king returned to his palace and spent the night without eating, drinking, or talking to anyone. He did not sleep all night.

The next morning King Darius rushed down to the den of lions. He yelled into the cave, "Daniel, has the God that you prayed to saved you from the lions?"

Much to the king's surprise, Daniel's voice came back, "O king, my God sent an angel and He shut the mouths of the lions. They have not hurt me."

The king was overjoyed. He gave orders to lift Daniel from the den. Then King Darius wrote to all the people in his kingdom. He said that they must fear and respect the God of Daniel, for He was the living God. He had performed the miracle of rescuing Daniel from the lions' den.

MUSICAL INSTRUMENTS

Make musical instruments for a marching parade to celebrate Daniel's escape.

Drum:

Spray paint an empty oatmeal carton and let it dry. Punch a hole on each side 2"-3" below the top. Thread enough string through the hole so it can be hung around the child's neck as he marches along and beats on the drum.

Pie Pan Jangle:

Punch 4-6 holes around the edge of a disposable pie pan. Thread yarn or string through the holes and attach small bells. Have children jangle their instruments as they march along.

Shaker:

Fill an empty coffee can one-fourth full with small pebbles or beans. Cover it with a plastic lid. A child may shake it back and forth as he marches along.

Parade Flags:

Design flags using old pillowcases. With markers or paints, draw pictures or designs on the cases to represent God's army marching along. Sew a piece of yarn to the top and bottom of each pillowcase and tie it to a stick. Let children wave the flags as they march along.

Parade Streamers:

Tie several long, thin pieces of colorful crepe paper to a stick. Show children how to make circle eights with the streamers in the air as they march along.

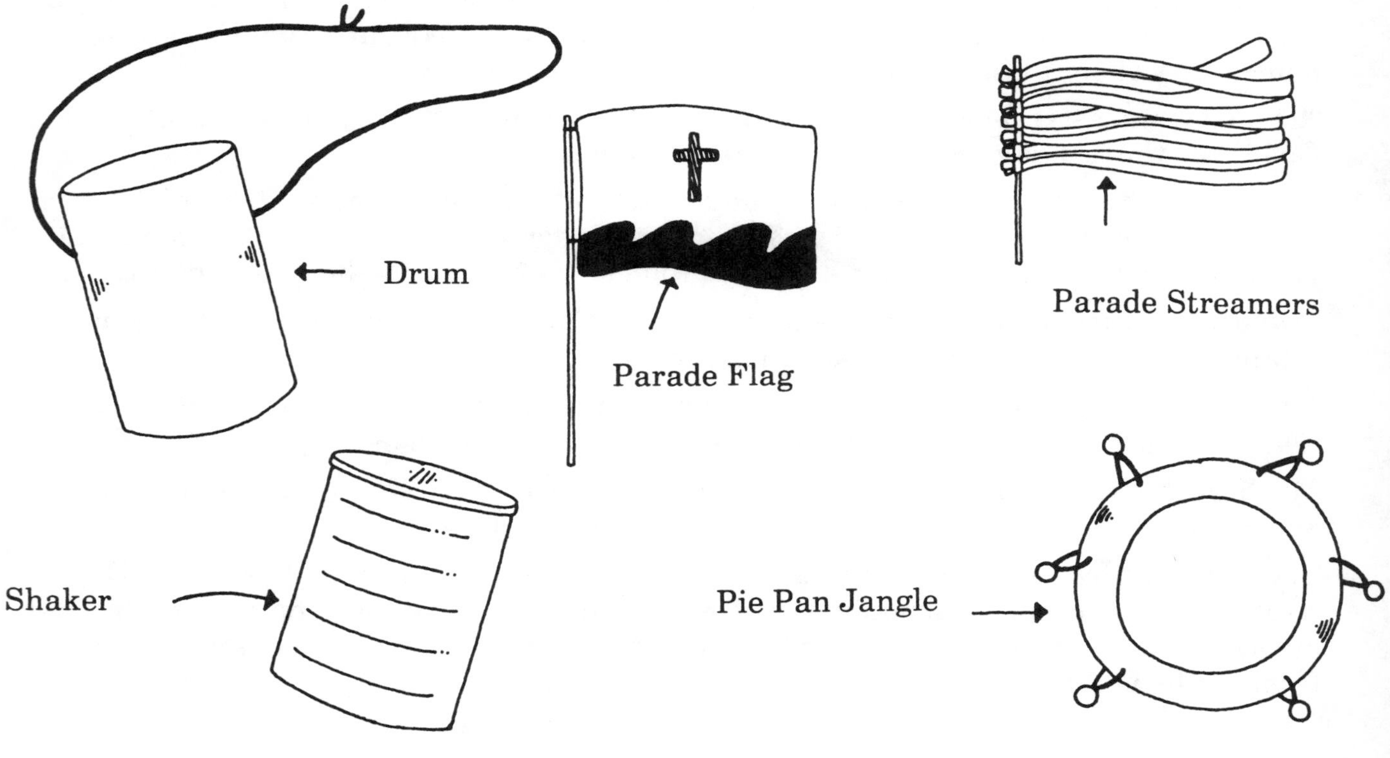

Drum
Parade Flag
Parade Streamers
Shaker
Pie Pan Jangle

IN THE MIDDLE OF THE DEN

Words by Phyllis Michael

Music by Helen Friesen

In the mid-dle of the den! In the mid-dle of the den! Yes, Dan-i-el
In the mid-dle of the den! In the mid-dle of the den! Well, Dan-i-el
In the mid-dle of the den! In the mid-dle of the den! God heard him
stood in the mid-dle of the den with big li-ons all a- round, hun-gry
prayed in the mid-dle of the den with those li-ons all a- round, hun-gry
pray in the mid-dle of the den with those li-ons all a- round, hun-gry
li-ons all a-round, Brave Dan-i-el stood in the mid-dle of the
li-ons all a-round, Brave Dan-i-el prayed in the mid-dle of the
li-ons all a-round, And God kept him safe in the mid-dle of the
den.
den.
den.
Chorus
God kept him safe! God kept him safe! Safe all right!

PUPPETS

Make puppets and act out the story of Daniel in the lions' den.

1. With scissors, colored papers, paste, and paints or markers, puppets may be made from lunch-sized paper bags. The bottom of the bag serves as the face and top portion of the mouth. The lower half of the mouth can be positioned under the flap so the puppet "talks" when the bottom of the bag is moved up and down.

2. Make a puppet by slipping a bag over a stick and stuffing the bag with wads of newspaper. Tie or staple the open end of the bag to the stick. Paint the head or glue paper "features" on to make a face. Use scrap yarn, wood shavings, buttons, etc., to decorate the puppets.

Tie yarn to form head and body.

3. For a larger puppet, stuff bags with wadded newspaper and staple or sew them shut with needle and thread. Start with the largest bag for the body. Staple or sew a medium-sized bag on top of the large bag for the head. Add bags for arms and legs, stapling open edges together after they're stuffed. When the puppet is formed, costume and decorate it any way you choose. Suspend the puppet by strings from a single stick, such as a yardstick. Jiggle the stick to make the puppet walk or move.

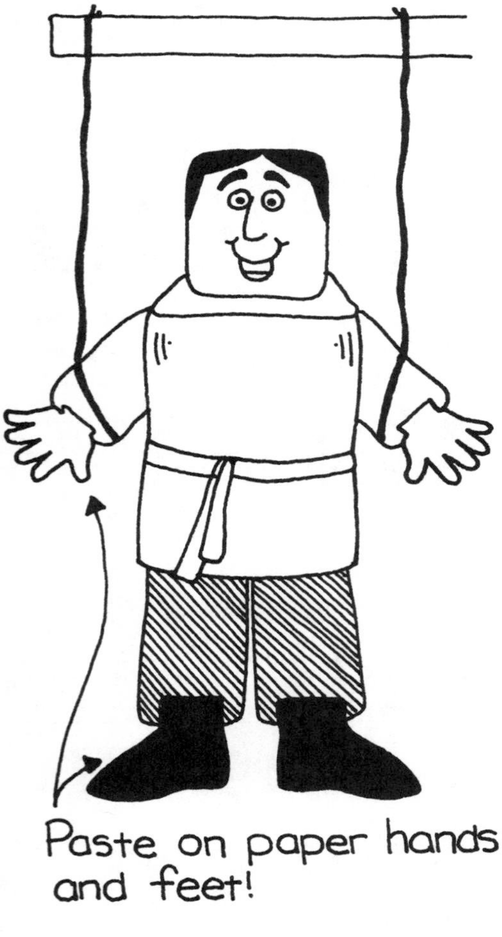
Paste on paper hands and feet!

4. To make a paper plate puppet, draw a lion's face on a paper plate. Glue 3" pieces of yarn around the plate. Cut two ears from construction paper and glue them on. Attach the plate to a stick or ruler. Make plate puppets for Daniel, the king, and an evil helper.

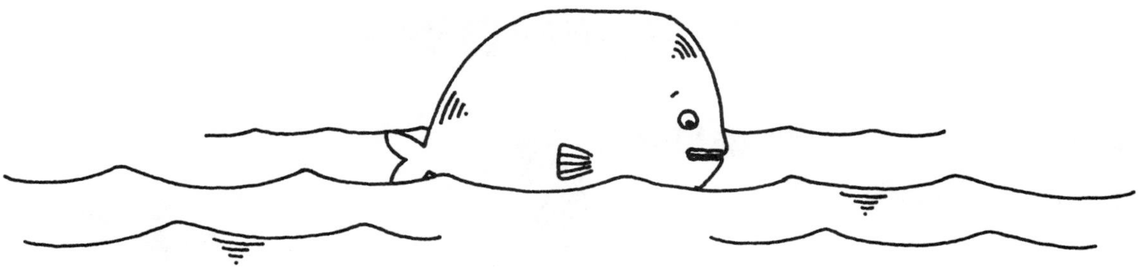

JONAH

Based on Jonah 1-3

One day God asked a man named Jonah to be His messenger. "Jonah, I want you to go to the great city of Nineveh and preach to the people there. They have been wicked."

Jonah knew about the evil people of Nineveh. They did not love God. They worshiped idols and committed many other sins. Jonah did not want to preach to them. He did not want to be God's messenger, so he ran away.

Jonah found a ship going to a place far away in Spain. He quickly got on board. Soon after the ship had moved out to sea, Jonah went below deck, lay down, and fell into a deep sleep.

As the ship moved farther out in the sea, the Lord sent a great wind on the sea, and a terrible storm came up. The ship thrashed around in the waves as if it would break apart.

The sailors were afraid. They called on their gods to make the storm stop, but the thrashing continued. Finally, the men went to Jonah. They shook him and asked, "Who is responsible for making all this trouble for us? Where do you come from?" The men were suspicious. "What is your country? From what people are you?"

Jonah answered, "I am a Hebrew and I worship the Lord, the God of heaven, who made the sea and the land." Jonah told them he was running away from the Lord.

The sea was getting rougher and rougher. "What should we do to make the sea calm down for us?" they asked.

Jonah answered, "Pick me up and throw me into the sea, and it will become calm. I know it's my fault this storm has come upon you."

The men did not want to throw Jonah overboard. They tried to row to shore but the wind only got wilder. They knew they would all die if they didn't do as Jonah said. The sailors prayed that they would be forgiven for taking a man's life, then they heaved Jonah over the side. At once the sea grew calm.

God did not let Jonah drown. He sent a huge fish to swallow him. While Jonah was inside the fish, he prayed to God. He asked God to forgive him for running away and for not preaching His Word to the sinful people of Nineveh. After three days and nights, the Lord commanded the fish, and it spit Jonah up onto dry land.

The Lord spoke to Jonah a second time, "Go to the great city of Nineveh and take the message that I send with you. Tell the people that I will destroy their city if they do not become sorry for their sins."

This time Jonah obeyed the Lord and went to Nineveh.

JONAH MOBILE

Materials:

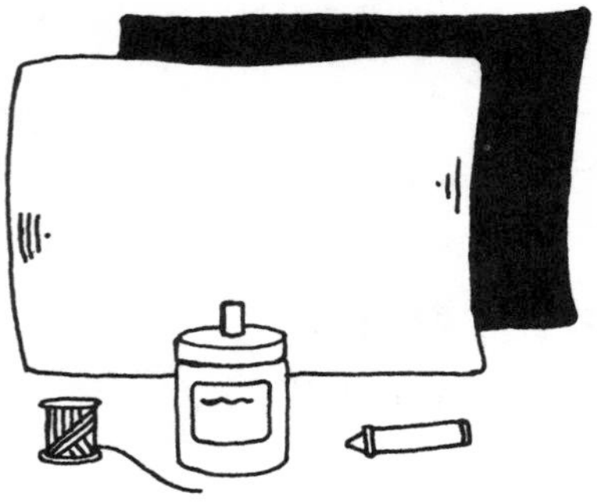

Construction paper
Glue
Scissors
Pencil
Thread

Directions:

Trace the fish below on black construction paper and cut it out. Trace the figure of Jonah on another color of construction paper and cut it out. Place Jonah in the open center of the fish. Glue a long piece of thread to the back of Jonah and the upper portion of the fish as illustrated. Allow at least 6" of thread above the fish for hanging.

THE SAVIOR IS BORN

Based on Luke 1:26-38; Matthew 1:18-24; Luke 2:1-20

One day Mary, a young girl in the village of Nazareth, was busy working in her family's house. She was thinking about her engagement to Joseph, a carpenter, when an angel appeared!

"Rejoice, you who are highly favored!" said the angel. "The Lord is with you."

At first, Mary didn't understand, but the angel said, "Do not be afraid, Mary. You have found favor with God. You will have a son, and you are to give Him the name Jesus. He will be great and will be called the Son of the Most High."

"I am the Lord's servant," answered Mary. "May it be as you have said." Then the angel left her.

At first, Joseph was upset at the news that Mary was expecting a child. Then an angel of the Lord appeared to him in a dream. The angel said, "Joseph, son of David, do not be afraid to take Mary home as your wife. She will give birth to a son, and you are to give Him the name Jesus, because He will save His people from their sins."

When Joseph woke up, he did what the angel of the Lord had commanded him, and took Mary to be his wife.

At that time the ruler of the Roman Empire issued a decree that a census should be taken of all people. Joseph and Mary left Nazareth and traveled to Bethlehem to be counted.

The trip down the long, dusty, dirt path was bumpy. Mary must have been uncomfortable as she rode on the donkey's back.

"Is the time near for the child to be born?" asked Joseph. "I'm afraid Bethlehem is so full of people, there may be nowhere to stay."

They stopped at each inn along the way. The innkeepers shook their heads and said, "Sorry, there isn't a room left in the entire city."

Finally, a kind man said they could stay in a nearby stable. That night Mary gave birth to a baby boy, and named Him Jesus. She wrapped the tiny child in cloth and laid Him in a bed of straw.

In a nearby field there were shepherds keeping watch over their flocks. An angel of the Lord appeared to them. "Don't be afraid," the angel assured them. "I'm here to tell you about some wonderful news. It's news for all people. Today in the town of David, a Savior has been born. He is Christ the Lord. You will know Him by this sign: You will find a baby wrapped in cloths and lying in a manger." Suddenly there were many angels in the sky, praising God.

When the angels disappeared the shepherds said, "Let's go to Bethlehem and see this thing that has happened, which the Lord has told us about." They hurried off and found Mary and Joseph and the baby lying in a manger.

Once the shepherds saw the tiny baby lying so peacefully in the hay, they praised God. Then they left and went to tell others the good news about the newborn child and what the angel had said. All who heard what the shepherds said were amazed.

ADVENT ACTIVITIES

Do the activities listed below, beginning December 1, to celebrate Advent.

1. Make an Advent wreath (see instructions on page 41).
2. Light one candle on the wreath. Read Romans 13:11-12.
3. Make a family tree by tracing handprints on green construction paper. Roll up the fingers slightly. Line up the hands in the shape of a tree and glue them on poster board. Add a gold star on top.
4. Make personalized Christmas balls using construction paper. Write each family member's name in glitter on a construction paper circle. Tie a bow with thin ribbon or yarn, and glue it on the family handprint tree.
5. Cover a large Styrofoam™ ball with mistletoe. Hang it above your door. Give people kisses of peace as they enter your home.
6. Cut the letters HAPPY BIRTHDAY, JESUS from colorful magazine pages. Hang them in the window.
7. Look at last year's Christmas cards. Pray for those who sent them.
8. Light the second candle on the wreath. Read Matthew 3:3.
9. Make Christmas cards for friends and family.
10. Go shopping together for a Christmas tree. Enjoy hot apple cider while sharing your favorite things about Christmas.
11. Sing Christmas songs as you bake Christmas goodies for friends.
12. Talk about the important gifts you have received. Visit a friend in need, sharing some of your homemade goodies.
13. Make Christmas tree decorations by cutting out scenes from last year's Christmas cards. Punch a hole in the top and tie each with a piece of yarn. As this year's Christmas cards arrive, share them with the family each evening.
14. Light the third candle on the wreath. String popcorn for a Christmas tree decoration.
15. Talk about memories of past Christmases. Paint a shoe box to be used for a Nativity scene.
16. Decorate the box with straw or small pieces of evergreen. Color and cut out the figure of the donkey (page 42) and place it in the stable.
17. Color and cut out the figure of Joseph (page 41) and place it in the stable. Read Matthew 1:18-24.
18. Color and glue glitter on the figure of the angel (page 41). Cut it out and glue it above the shoe box. Read Luke 1:26-28.
19. Color and cut out the figure of Mary (page 41) and place it in the stable. Read Luke 1:29-38.
20. Color and cut out the lamb (page 41), glue on white cotton, and place it in the stable. Read Luke 2:1-7.
21. Color the star (page 42) yellow, glue gold glitter on it, and cut it out. Glue it above the stable. Read Luke 2:8-14.
22. Color and cut out the figure of the shepherd (page 42) and place it in the stable. Read Luke 2:15-20.
23. Color and cut out the figures of the wise men (page 42) and place them in the stable. Read Matthew 2:1-12.
24. Light the fourth candle on the wreath. Color and cut out the figure of Jesus (page 41) and place it in the stable. Join hands and sing happy birthday to Jesus.
25. Before opening Christmas gifts, have a short worship and prayer time.

After Christmas is over, write a thank-You note to God.

ADVENT WREATH

To make an Advent wreath, press four candles into a Styrofoam™ wreath so they stand an equal distance from each other. Glue silk or plastic greenery around the top of the wreath.

PATTERNS

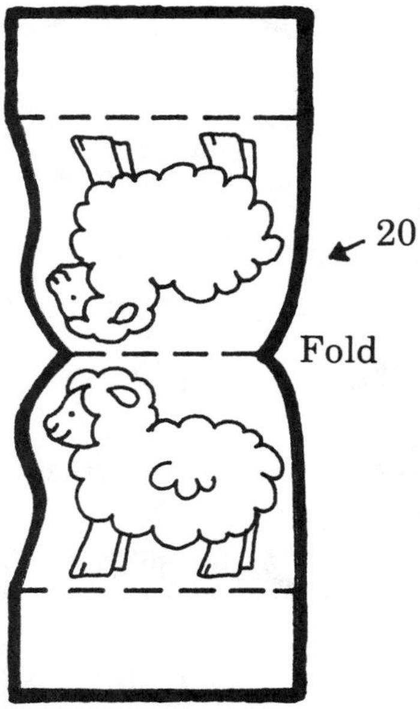
20
Fold

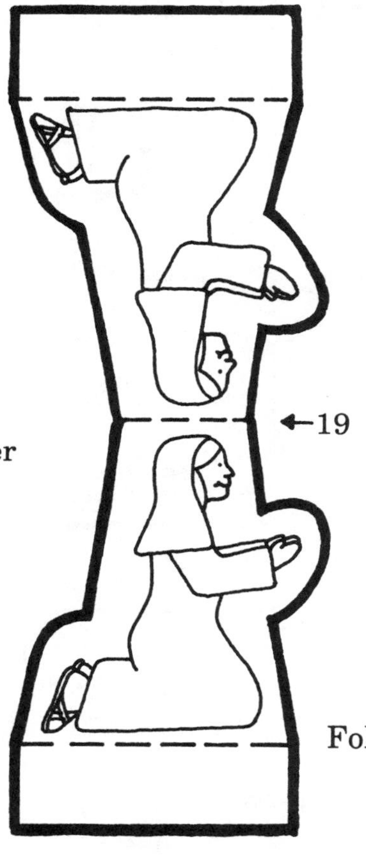
19
Fold under

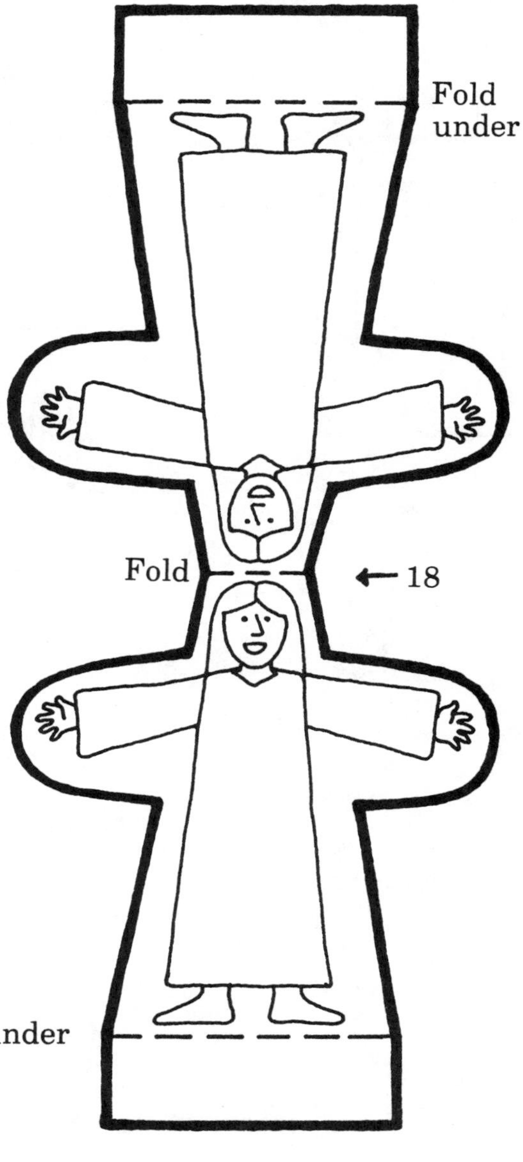
Fold under
Fold
18
Fold under

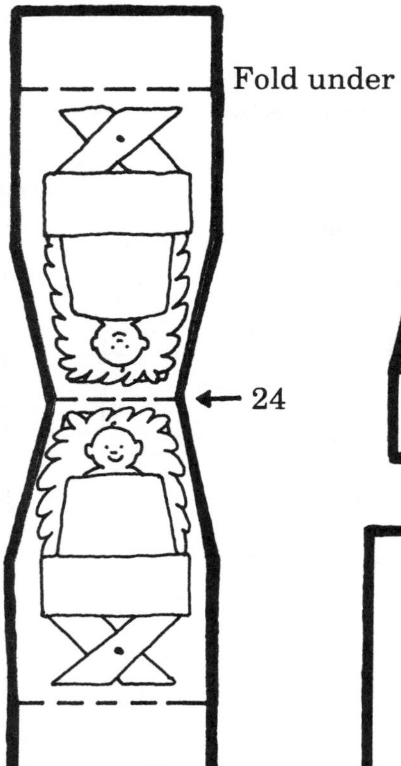
Fold under
24

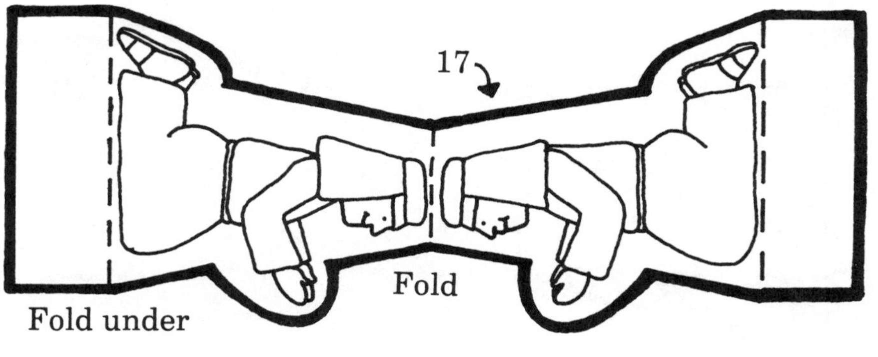
17
Fold
Fold under

PATTERNS

16

Fold under

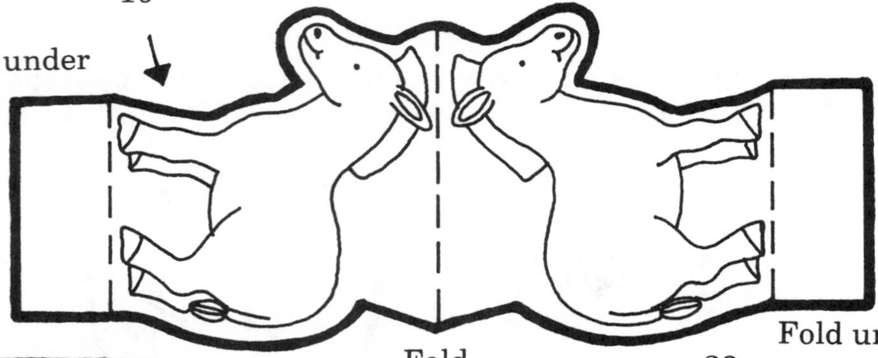

Fold

Fold under

21

23

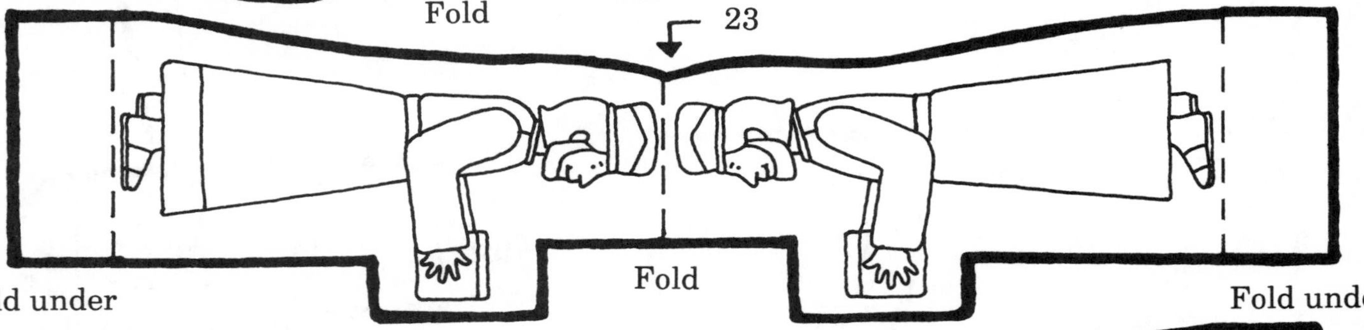

Fold

Fold under

Fold under

23

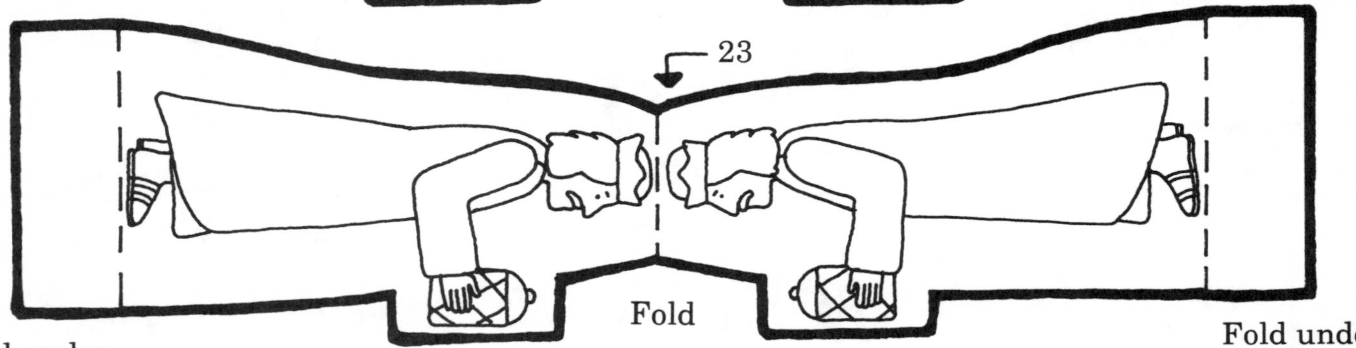

Fold

Fold under

Fold under

23

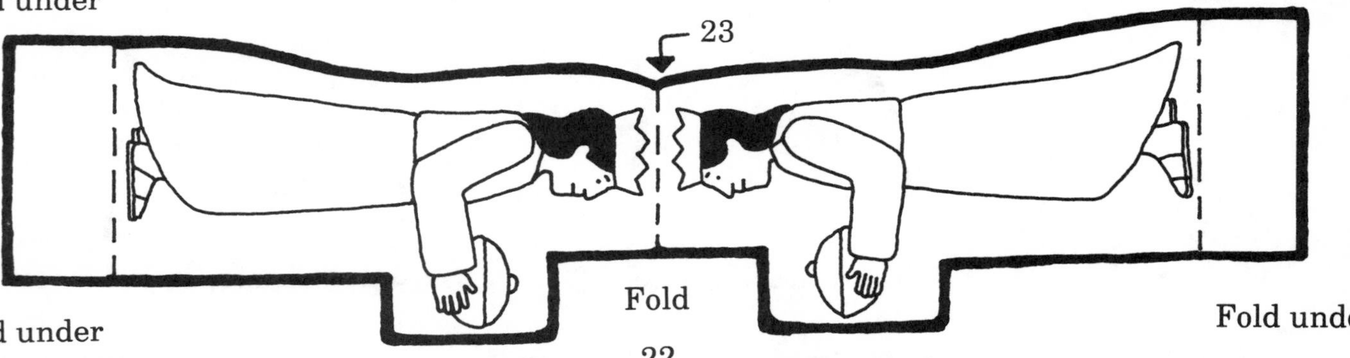

Fold

Fold under

Fold under

22

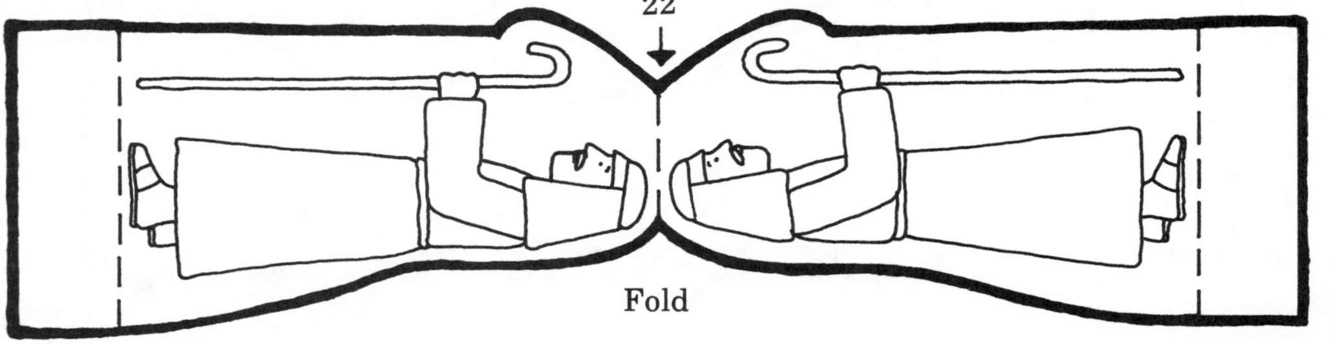

Fold

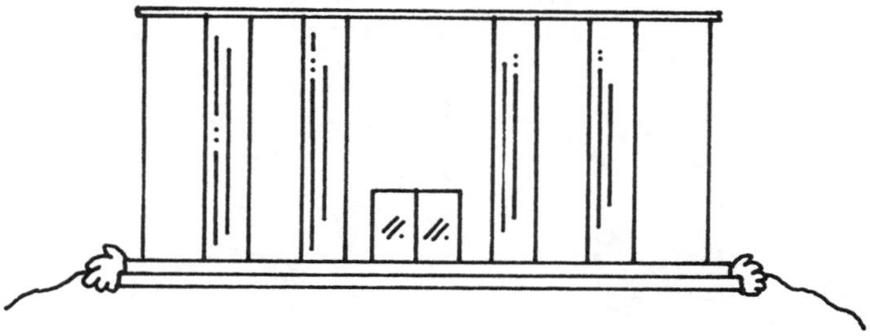

A VISIT TO THE TEMPLE

Based on Luke 2:41-52

Mary and Joseph watched their son Jesus grow up quickly. He learned to crawl, and walk and talk just like other children. He liked to play games like other children too. Whatever His parents asked Him to do, He did happily. Most of all, Jesus loved to hear the Old Testament stories. Mary told Him about what God had done in the "old" days. With each story, Jesus wanted to learn more.

Every year Mary and Joseph traveled to Jerusalem to celebrate the Feast of the Passover. It reminded the people of the day when God had rescued the Israelites from Pharaoh and had led His people out of Egypt.

When Jesus was twelve years old, He went with His parents to join in the celebration. For the first time, Jesus was allowed to eat the Passover dinner and go to the special services in the temple.

After the services were over, many people went through the city streets shopping in the markets and visiting old friends and neighbors. Jesus wanted most to hear the Word of God, so He stayed in the temple and talked to the teachers of the Law, asking them to tell Him more.

When the week of celebration was over, the families packed up their belongings and began walking back to their homes. After a day of traveling, Mary and Joseph discovered that Jesus was not with them. "We must go back to Jerusalem and find Him," said Joseph, turning to walk back to the city.

After hours of walking, tired Mary and Joseph arrived back in Jerusalem. They frantically asked storekeepers and people in the street. Three days had passed since they had last seen Jesus.

Finally, Mary and Joseph went to the temple and saw Jesus sitting with the teachers, listening carefully and asking questions. Everyone was amazed at the boy's understanding of God and His Word.

Mary asked her son, "What are You doing? We have been looking for You for three days. We've been so worried!"

Jesus said, "Why were you looking for Me? Didn't you know that I would be in My Father's house?" But Mary and Joseph did not understand what He was saying to them.

Jesus left with them and went down to Nazareth. There He continued to grow and learn more about the Word of God.

I'll be Joseph!
And I'll be Mary!

THE BOY JESUS IN THE TEMPLE

(A Play)

Welcome to Our Play!

Cast of characters:

- Jesus
- Mary
- Joseph
- Friends of Mary and Joseph
- Townspeople
- Wise teachers

Narrator: The time has come for You to go to the big city and see the temple.

Mary: Come with us, Jesus, to Jerusalem.

Jesus: I would love to go to Jerusalem and see the temple!

Narrator: It was a long walk to Jerusalem. (Mary, Joseph, Jesus, and townspeople walk.)

Mary: At last we have come to the big city.

Joseph: Let us go to the temple to pray and sing and hear God's Word.

Jesus: (Looking around the temple) Oh how big the temple is, and how beautiful!

Narrator: Jesus sat among the wise teachers and listened to them speak of God. How surprised the teachers were when they heard the things Jesus knew.

Teacher 1: How wise this young boy is.

Teacher 2: He knows so many things about God's Word.

Narrator: Jesus stayed in Jerusalem for seven days. When they started home, they thought Jesus was with them, walking with His friends. When time passed and Jesus did not come to them, they began to worry.

Joseph: Mary, have you seen Jesus? He did not eat with us or sleep with us. Is He with some friends?

Mary: Oh my. Where can He be? (to friends) Have you seen our son Jesus? We cannot find Him.

Joseph:	We must look for Him until we find Him. We shall go back to Jerusalem and search for Him there.
Narrator:	Mary and Joseph were very worried as they hurried back to Jerusalem. When they arrived, they were tired and afraid. They began stopping people in the streets and knocking on doors.
Joseph:	(Knocking on door) Have you seen a boy, twelve years old, this high . . . ?
Townsperson:	No, I have seen no one.
Mary:	(Knocking on door) Have you seen a boy? He is our son . . . .
Townsperson:	I was at the temple today. There was a boy there. A very wise boy talking about heaven and earth.
Narrator:	Mary and Joseph rushed to the temple, praying that Jesus would be there. When they arrived they found their son sitting with the wise teachers.
Mary:	Jesus, why did You do this? We have looked everywhere for You.
Joseph:	When we could not find You, we thought You were lost.
Mary:	We were so worried about You.
Jesus:	God is My Father. I was doing His work. Didn't you know that I had to be here in My Father's house?
Narrator:	Then Jesus left the temple. He went home with Mary and Joseph. Jesus continued to grow in wisdom. Mary often thought about her son, Jesus. She knew He was very special.
Mary:	I will always remember how glad Jesus was to hear the Word of God in the temple.

God is My Father.
I was doing His work.

SPAGHETTI SCULPTURE

spaghetti noodles
glue
aluminum foil

Materials:

Spaghetti
White glue
Food coloring
Aluminum foil
String

Directions:

1. Cook spaghetti about 8 minutes, drain, and rinse.
2. Tint $1/8$ cup of white glue with food coloring. Place a handful of spaghetti in this mixture and move around until well covered. Combine colors for an interesting variation.
3. Place spaghetti on a piece of foil and form a dove shape. Be sure the spaghetti overlaps. Bend foil up on edges so the glue doesn't run off. Allow it to dry for several days.
4. Hang the sculptures. Notice the stained glass quality when the light sparkles through.

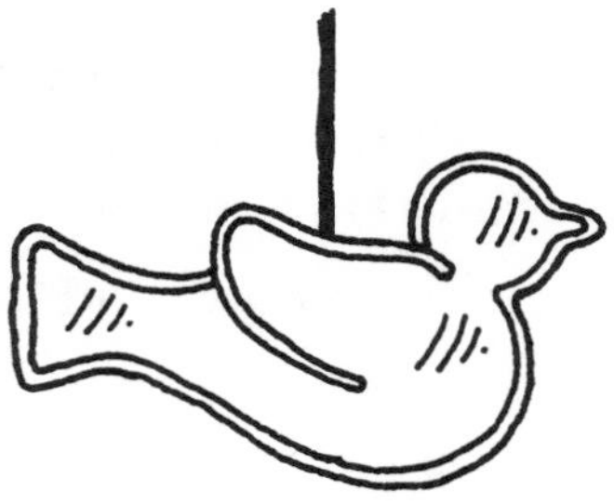

HIDE THE BOOKMARK

Before class make a bookmark and write "Study God's Word" on it. Hide the bookmark.

After telling the story of Jesus at the temple, talk about how Mary and Joseph thought Jesus was lost. Tell the children that you, also, have lost something. It's a bookmark. Where could it be? At first, don't give the children any clues. Ask if they have any ideas about how you might find it. Talk about how Mary and Joseph may have felt when they were trying to find Jesus. Mary and Joseph retraced their steps. Have the children retrace your steps until they find the bookmark.

Ask the children what words are on the bookmark. Talk about how Mary and Joseph found Jesus studying God's Word.

Let the children take turns hiding the bookmark and giving clues, such as "hot" and "cold," while other children try to find it.

Study God's Word

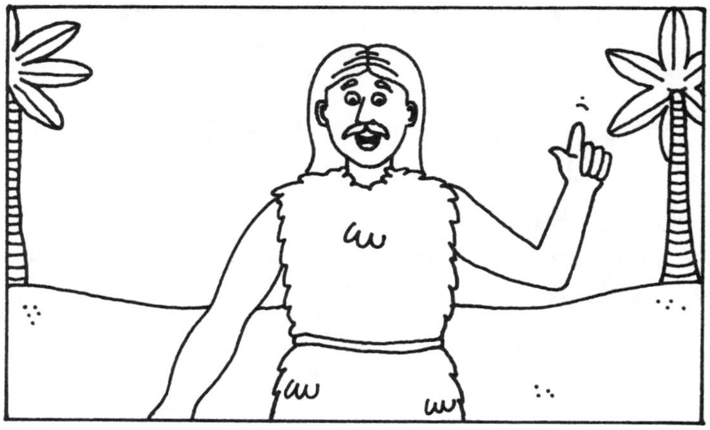

JESUS IS BAPTIZED

Based on Matthew 3:13-17; Mark 1:4-11

A loud voice rang out across the wilderness: "Repent and be baptized. Prepare the way for the Lord!" People gathered around a strange-looking man who was dressed in clothes made of camel's hair. His voice grew loud and excited as he talked to them. Word spread about this man named John the Baptist who wandered across the desert eating locusts and wild honey.

People were used to going to the temple to study the Word of God. This man was not at all like the teachers and priests they had known. A man yelled from the crowd, "Are you the Messiah? Are you the one that God is going to send to deliver us?"

John's voice grew quieter as the crowd stared. "No," John said, "I am not good enough to be a slave to the one God is sending."

John walked out into the Jordan River and stood in the water. "Come," he yelled to the onlookers, "Repent, and be baptized!"

All sorts of people followed John into the water. Soldiers put down their weapons and waded out. Tax collectors came and asked, "What are we to do?" John spoke gently, "Don't take poor people's money to pay high taxes."

The crowds continued to grow as John called on them to ask for God's forgiveness. One day as John stood preaching to a crowd, he suddenly grew silent. He felt someone watching him. He turned to see Jesus standing nearby. "Look," said John pointing to Jesus, "Here He comes. This is the Lamb of God. The one I have spoken to you about. He will give Himself as a sacrifice to take away the sins of the world!"

Jesus walked toward John and placed His hand on John's shoulder. "Baptize Me," He said.

John quickly shook his head. "Oh no, You should be the one who baptizes me," he said.

"Do as I say," said Jesus, "It is My Father's will."

John and Jesus went together out into the Jordan River. As soon as He was baptized, Jesus' face began to shine. The crowd became still as the heavens opened. The Holy Spirit, in the form of a dove, came down upon Jesus. The people stared in amazement as the voice of God spoke. "This is My Son, whom I love; with Him I am well pleased."

WHERE IS JOHN?

Sing this variation of the old familiar song, "Where Is Thumbkin?" Use markers to draw a face on each of your thumbs and fingers.

Put your hands behind your back. Bring out your right thumb for John as you sing the second line of the first stanza. Bring out the left thumb for Jesus as you sing the second line of the second stanza.

On the second line of the last stanza, wiggle the rest of your fingers for the people. Bring the fingers together and fold your hands as if praying for the final line, "Praise to God."

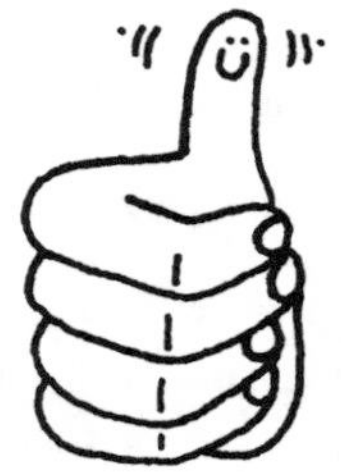

Where is John? Where is John?
Here I am. Here I am.
Near the River Jordan,
Near the River Jordan,
Baptizing. Baptizing.

Where is Jesus? Where is Jesus?
Here I am. Here I am.
Coming to the river,
Coming to the river,
Baptize Me. Baptize Me.

Where are the people? Where are the people?
Here we are. Here we are.
Coming to the river,
Coming to the river,
Praise to God. Praise to God.

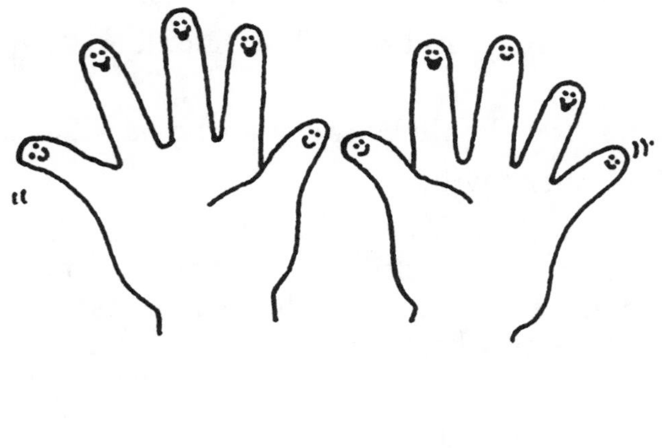

PETER'S CATCH OF FISH

Based on Luke 5:1-11

It was very early in the morning. Out on the Sea of Galilee were boats full of men trying to catch some fish.

"We might as well pull up our nets and go in," called Peter, one of the disappointed fishermen. "We have been out here all night. We have not caught a single fish!"

Andrew, Peter's brother, hauled in the net and exclaimed. "From the looks of this net, the only things we caught were rocks and sand." He carefully examined it. "It will take a lot of hard work to get this cleaned up."

"Call over to the other boat," said Peter. "Tell James and John we're going in to shore. Perhaps another time will be better."

When the boats reached shore, the fishermen saw Jesus walking along the beach. Hundreds of people were following Him, waiting to hear Him teach God's Word. Jesus approached Peter and asked if He might use his boat. "Take Me out a little way from shore so I will be able to see all the people better," Jesus said.

Peter was happy to help the Master. He listened carefully as Jesus sat and talked about God's wisdom and love. When Jesus had finished speaking, the people went back to their homes or work. Then the Lord turned to Peter and said, "Take the boat out into deep water, and let the nets down for a catch."

Peter was an expert fisherman. He knew the best place to fish was along the shore, not the deep water. He also felt the sunlight on his cheeks, and wondered why they would fish in the daytime. All fishermen knew that the nighttime was the best time for catching fish. But Peter obeyed.

Peter and Andrew unfolded their net and dropped it into the deep sea. When they tried pulling it up, they realized it was heavy with fish. "Call James and John," cried Peter. "We must have help to bring in all these fish. Our net will surely break!"

The two brothers came in their boat, and together the four of them pulled and tugged. At last the heavy net was pulled in. Soon both boats were so full they began to sink.

When Peter saw this great miracle of Jesus, he fell down on his knees. Jesus laid His hand on Peter's shoulder and said, "From now on, you will catch men."

The fishermen pulled their boats up on shore, left everything, and followed Jesus.

3-D FISH

Materials:

Butcher paper
Paper clips
Colored construction paper
Scissors
Glue
Scrap paper
Stick
Marker
Yarn
Crayons
Magnet
Stapler (optional)

Directions:

1. Copy and cut out the large fish shape on page 51.
2. Use a crayon to lightly trace the fish on construction paper.
3. Add a second sheet and cut two fish out.
4. Glue the sides together, leaving a 6" opening near the back end.
5. Stuff with scrap paper. Glue the opening closed. (A few staples may be needed to close the opening.)
6. Attach a paper clip to the top of the fish.

Color a large sheet of butcher paper blue; then lay it on the floor to represent the ocean. Tie a piece of yarn to a stick for a fishing pole. Attach a magnet to the end of the yarn. Toss several fish onto the butcher paper and take turns trying to "catch" them.

When the "fishing" is over, print "I will make you fishers of men" across the butcher paper, and hang it on the wall. (You may want to color in some seaweed and other fish.) Attach a piece of yarn to each fish and hang it from the ceiling in front of the "ocean" for a three-dimensional bulletin board.

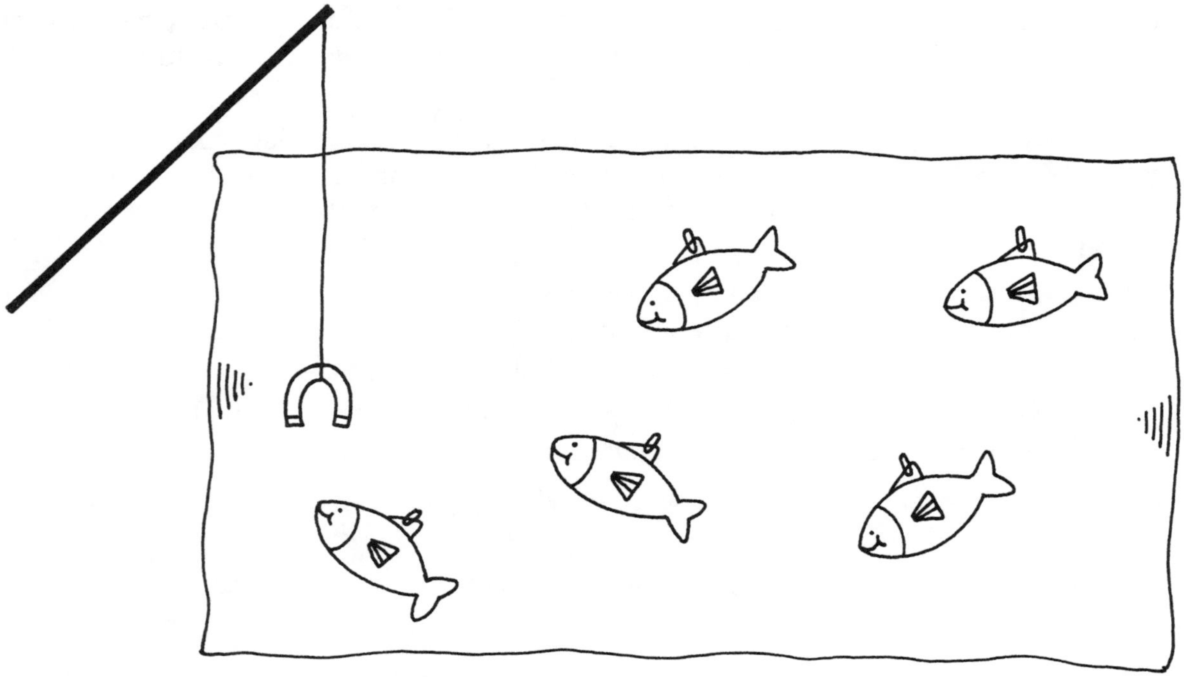

FISH PATTERN

I WILL MAKE YOU FISHERS OF MEN

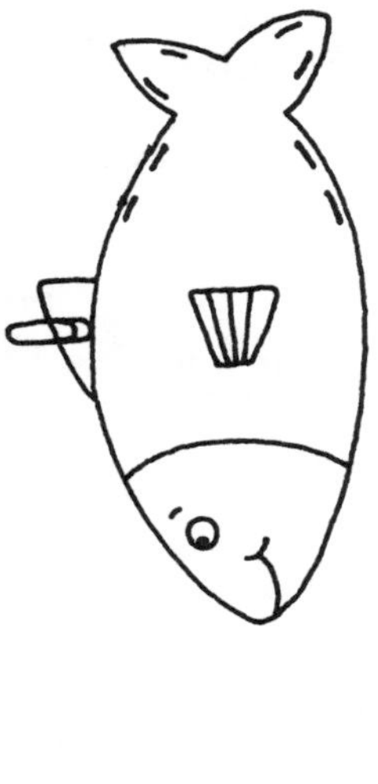

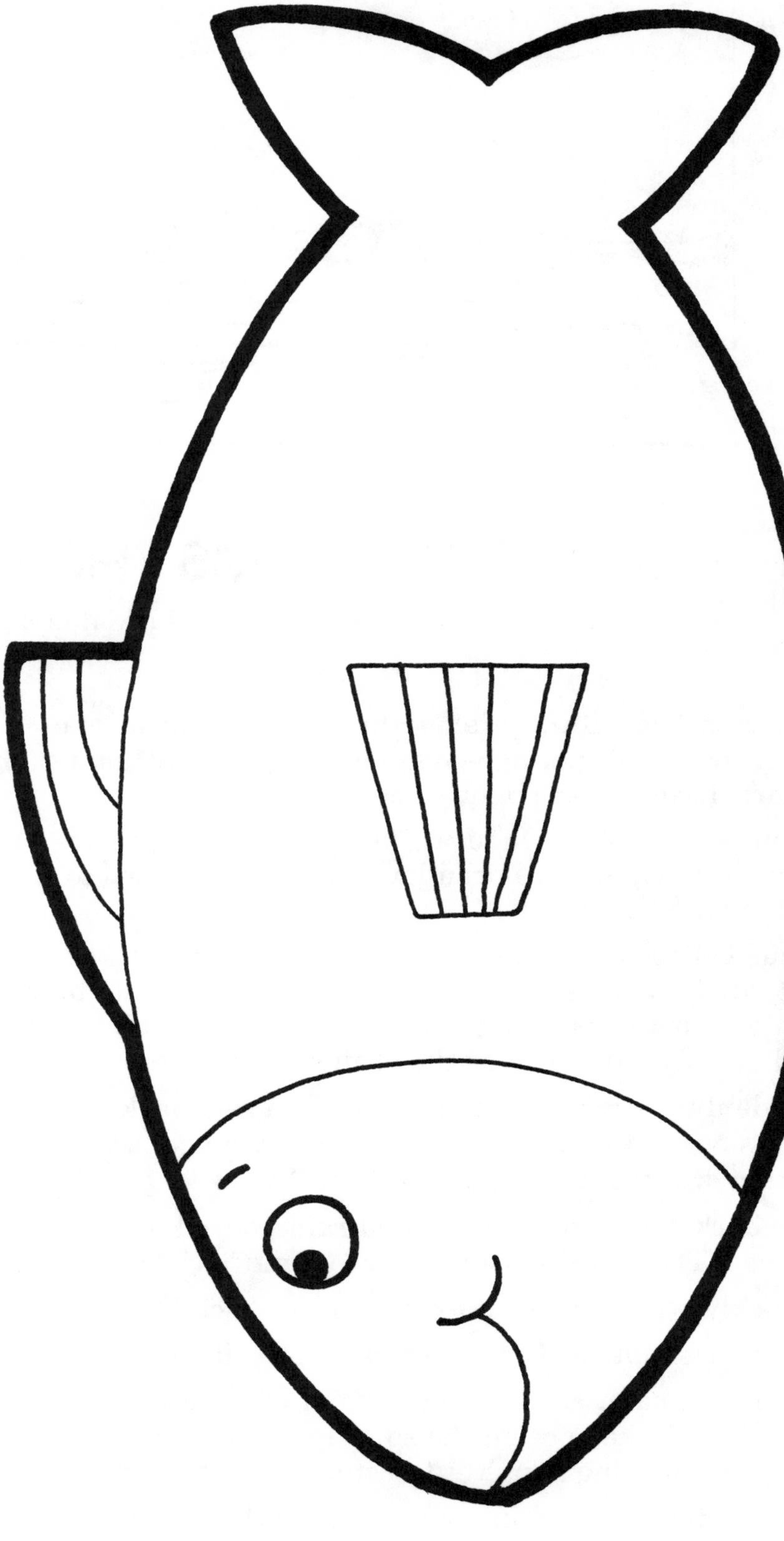

JESUS CALMS THE STORM

Based on Matthew 8:23-27; Mark 4:35-41; Luke 8:22-25

It was a beautiful, quiet night. Jesus stood at the shore of the Sea of Galilee. He listened to the rippling waves gently splashing against the small boats anchored at the wharf. They rocked slightly back and forth.

Jesus was tired. He had worked hard talking to the large crowds of people that day. Men, women, and children had traveled for miles to hear Him preach God's Word and watch Him heal the sick.

Jesus called to His disciples, "Let's go over to the other side of the lake." His friends untied the boat and lifted the sails. As the soft breeze touched the cloth, the boat floated out to sea. The gentle rocking soothed Jesus. He went to the back of the boat and quickly fell asleep as they sailed out into the sea.

Suddenly, without warning, the sky grew dark. A large, black cloud appeared. The waves began to roll higher. Water crashed against the sides of the boat. The men yelled as they worked to bring the sails in, "We're all going to die in this storm!"

The dark clouds burst open and rain poured down, throwing the boat farther out into the sea. The mens' arms ached as they tried to row the boat to shore.

"Quickly, wake Jesus!" cried one of the disciples.

The men shouted, "Lord, save us! We're all going to die!" And Jesus woke up.

Jesus was calm as He replied, "You of little faith, why are you so afraid?" Slowly He stood and looked out on the sea. He scolded the winds and the waves. Just like a child ashamed of being naughty, the storm quieted and the seas became calm.

The disciples gasped in amazement. "What kind of man is this?" they asked. "Even the winds and the waves obey Him!"

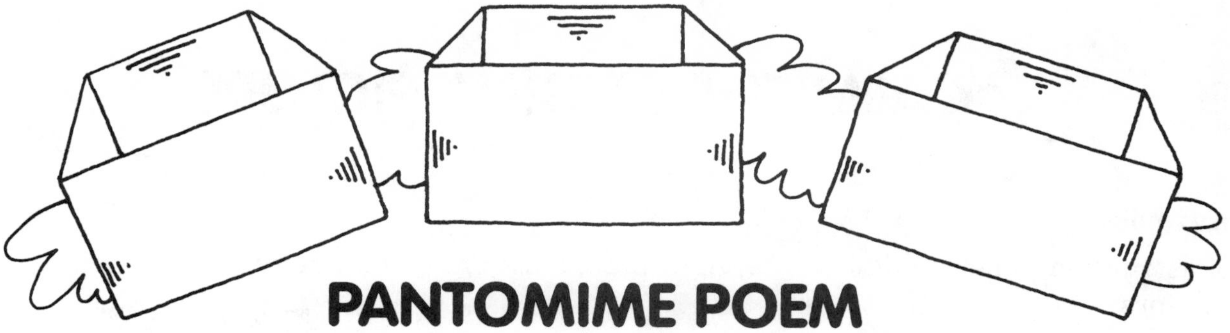

PANTOMIME POEM

Directions:

Staple several large cardboard boxes together to form a boat. Have the children stand in the boxes and pretend to be the disciples on that night when Jesus calmed the sea. Practice the poem together. Choose one child to be Jesus and several others to be the disciples. Children that are not chosen for special parts may recite the poem while the others act it out.

It was calm upon the sea.
The moon and stars shone bright.
When Jesus and His disciples
Set sail that quiet night.

Disciples look up at the sky and smile.

Then all at once the lightning flashed!
A cloud burst overhead.
The waves began to tumble.
The men cried, "We'll all be dead!"

Disciples cover their heads and move boxes back and forth.

But Jesus called out to the storm,
"Be calm; obey My will."
The disciples stood in wonder
As the wind and waves grew still.

Jesus stands and points to the sky. Everything is still.

"CALM THE STORM" PICTURE

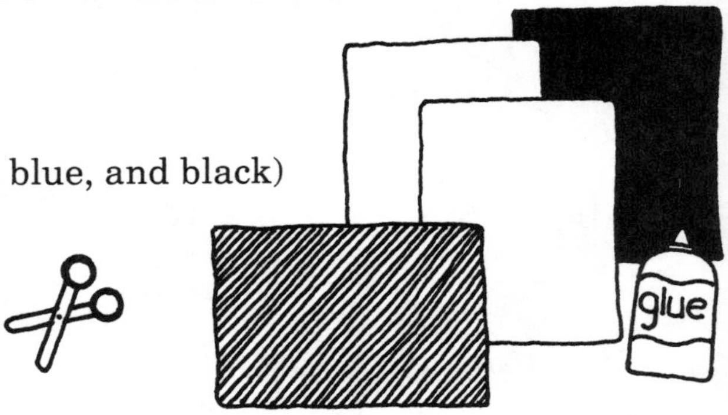
glue

Materials:

Construction paper (yellow, white, light blue, dark blue, and black)
Scissors
Glue
Pencil

Directions:

Copy the patterns on pages 55-56 on construction paper and cut them out.

Use a full sheet of light blue construction paper for the background. Fold back the top of the paper 1 1/2". Fold back the bottom 1 1/2". With the two edges folded back, glue on the white cloud, yellow moon, and blue waves as shown. Glue the boat in the center.

Unfold the paper and glue the lightning, black cloud, and blue waves on the back of the folded pieces.

Glue the poem to the back of the picture. Read the poem and open and close the folds to illustrate the story.

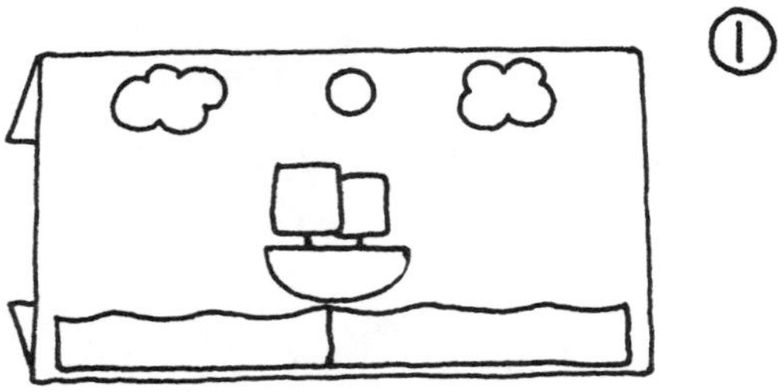

It was calm upon the sea.
The moon and stars shone bright.
When Jesus and His disciples
Set sail that quiet night.

Then all at once the lightning flashed!
A cloud burst overhead.
The waves began to tumble.
The men cried, "We'll all be dead!"

But Jesus called out to the storm,
"Be calm; obey My will."
The disciples stood in wonder
As the wind and waves grew still.

"JESUS CALMS THE STORM" PATTERNS

"JESUS CALMS THE STORM" PATTERNS

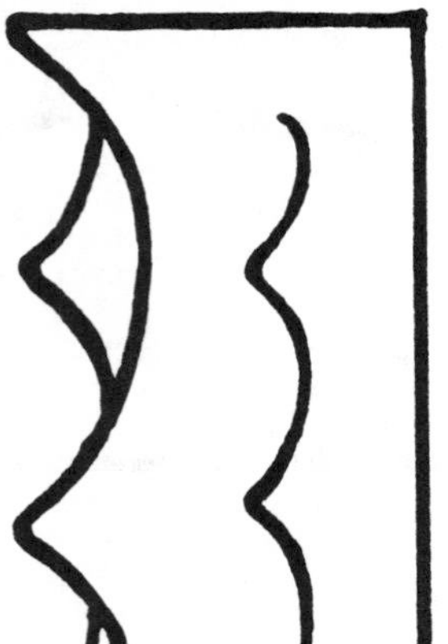

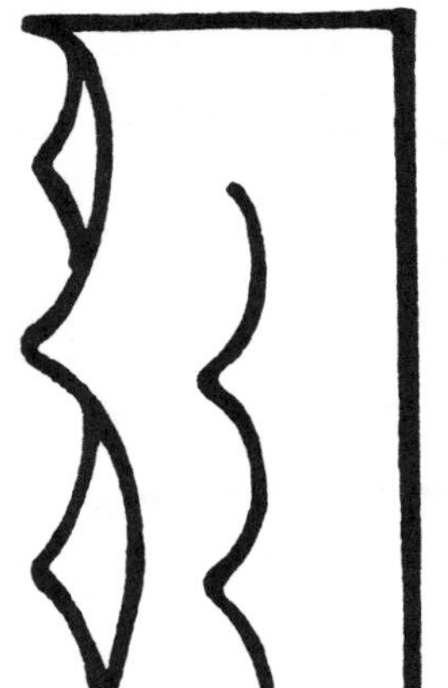

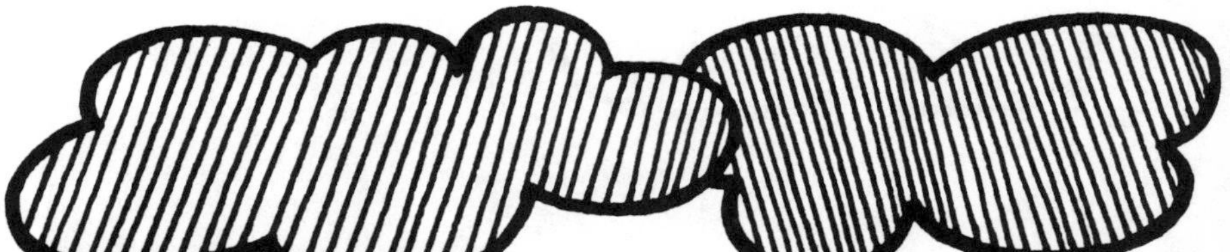

JAIRUS' ANSWERED PRAYER

Based on Mark 5:21-43

Jairus' daughter was dying. He was desperate to save his child's life, so he set out to find Jesus, the man they called the miracle worker. Jairus traveled through the night to Galilee, searching. He would find Jesus and bring Him back! The miracle worker would make his daughter well.

Jairus' legs ached from the many miles he had walked, but he didn't stop to rest. Each step brought him closer. Finally he saw a crowd ahead. Voices called out from the hillside. "It's the one they call Jesus. He's here, the one who heals the crippled!"

Jairus rushed toward the crowd, pushing and shoving. He cried out for them to let him pass. "My daughter; she's dying . . . please!" Suddenly, Jarius pushed himself into the crowd and fell down in the dirt. He peered up and saw a man looking thoughtfully at him. Jairus paused for a moment in wonder. It was Jesus!

Jairus stuttered as he began frantically telling Jesus about his child. "Twelve years old, she is sick . . . so sick . . . she's dying. Please come, she'll die . . . there's no one else. You must come. Put Your hands on her so she will be healed and live."

His pleading eyes met Jesus' eyes–so gentle, so kind. Jairus knew He would come.

Suddenly a man from the house of Jairus appeared. His face was filled with grief, and his head was low. He quietly said, "Jairus, your daughter is dead." He put his arm around the stunned father. "Don't bother the teacher anymore."

A cold chill raced through Jairus. Jesus put His hand out and said, "Don't be afraid; just believe, and she will be healed." He continued on to the home of Jairus.

As they came near, they heard mourners wailing and mourning. Jesus called out, "Stop wailing. She is not dead, but sleeping."

Jesus' gentle eyes looked at the pale, lifeless girl. He reached out for the cold hand. Then He spoke: "My child, get up!"

Jairus stood frozen. His daughter's eyes blinked, and her head moved. She stood up and walked around!

"My little girl," cried Jairus. "My prayer has been answered. She lives! She lives!"

Jesus told him to feed the child, and to tell no one of the miracle. Then He left. There were so many others that needed Him.

MISSING MIRACLE

Have the children color the pictures of some of the miracles Jesus performed. Cut out the pictures and place them on the table faceup. Let children study them for a few minutes, then close their eyes as one picture is taken away. When the children open their eyes, they must guess which miracle is missing. Children may take turns removing the miracles.

Try taking away two miracles, then three. Can the children still guess which miracles are missing?

Feeding the Five Thousand

Calming of the Storm

Walking on Water

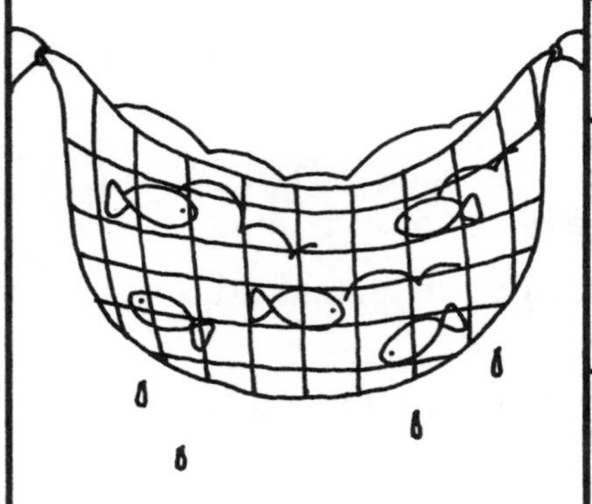

Catch of Fish

Healing Jairus' Daughter

Giving Sight to a Blind Man

THE GOOD SAMARITAN

Based on Luke 10:25-37

One day Jesus sat patiently talking to people, with His disciples sitting nearby. A man who was an expert in the law asked Jesus a question to try to trick Him. "What must I do to go to heaven?" the man asked.

Jesus knew that many people studied the Old Testament books of the Bible and knew all of God's laws by heart. They made sure other people obeyed these laws too. But Jesus also knew that these people didn't always practice the love of God. They didn't have the Lord in their hearts.

Jesus said to the man, "You know God's Law very well, don't you? Tell me what you have read."

The man answered quickly, "Love the Lord your God with all your heart and with all your soul and with all your strength and with all your mind, and love your neighbor as yourself."

"That's right," said Jesus. "Do that and you will go to heaven."

The man wanted Jesus to tell him more. "Who is my neighbor?" he asked.

Jesus answered the question by telling this story.

One day a man was traveling to Jericho on a dangerous, rocky path. A band of robbers attacked him. They beat him, took all his clothes, and left him beside the road to die.

After a while, a priest came by. He had been to the temple, teaching God's Law to people. He looked away and kept walking.

Next, a Levite came down the road. He also walked on without stopping.

Then the sounds of donkey hoofs could be heard. It was a Samaritan. Many Jewish people hated Samaritans. As this Samaritan came upon the hurt man, he didn't think about any hatred. He quickly got his travel bag from his donkey's side. He opened it and took out wine and oil. He tore his own clothes, soaked the cloth with wine, and carefully cleaned the man's wounds. He poured oil on the painful cuts to help them heal. Then he bandaged the wounds. The man was heavy, but the Samaritan pulled him up and lifted him onto his own donkey.

When they came to an inn, the Samaritan paid for a room and spent the whole night taking care of the hurt man. The next morning he gave the innkeeper two silver coins (as much as many people earned for two days of work). "Look after him," the Samaritan said, "and when I return, I will pay you for any other expenses."

When Jesus was done telling the story, He asked the law expert, "Which of these three men do you think was a neighbor to the man who fell into the hands of the robbers?"

The expert replied, "The one who had mercy on him."

Jesus told him, "Go and be like the Samaritan."

TENDER LOVING CARE

There are many people today who need our help. Can you think of some? How about the people that live in nursing homes? Can you think of how we might be able to help them? One way to show your love for others is to make cookies for them.

vanilla

TLC Cookies
(The dough can be made ahead of time.)

Mix together:
$^{3}/_{4}$ cup shortening (part butter)
1 cup sugar
2 eggs
1 teaspoon vanilla

Blend in:
$1^{1}/_{2}$ cups flour
1 teaspoon baking powder
1 teaspoon salt
Cover the dough; chill at least one hour.

Roll the dough $^{1}/_{8}$" thick on a lightly floured board. Cut out with a heart-shaped cookie cutter.

Mix with fork in a small bowl: 2 egg yolks, $^{1}/_{2}$ teaspoon water. Divide the mixture into small cups. Add a few drops of food color to each cup to make several different colors. Using a different paintbrush for each color, paint designs or messages on your cookies with tender loving care.

Bake at 350° for 6 to 8 minutes or until lightly brown; then cool.

Put the beautiful cookies in a cloth-lined basket and take them to a local nursing home. Share yourself and your cookies with your "neighbors."

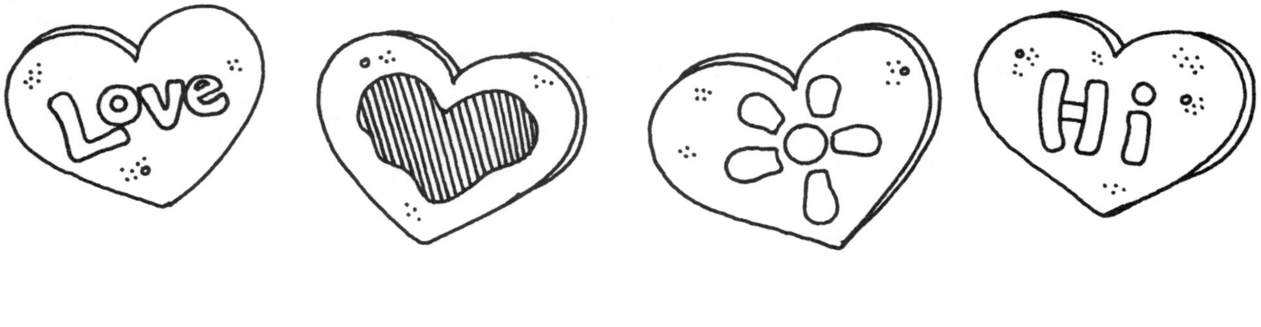
Love
Hi

THE KING

Based on Mark 11:1-11

The city of Jerusalem was full of excitement. It was time to celebrate the Feast of the Passover. People had come from miles around.

News spread that the King of the Jews was coming. Crowds began to close in–pushing, shoving, stretching their necks to see. The noise increased with the excitement, and soldiers attempted to calm the crowd. But the people only became more restless.

"He's coming!" someone shouted. "I see Him! The King, the King of the Jews!" The people began to wave palm branches as they called out, "Hosanna! Hosanna! Blessed is the King of Israel!"

A man riding on a donkey with a robe thrown over it came into view. But this man didn't look like a king. He didn't wear beautiful jewels. There was no crown on His head.

Someone called out, "Who is He?"

A voice from the excited crowd answered, "It is Jesus!"

As Jesus rode nearer, some of the people placed their palm leaves in the road. Others took off their robes and laid them in the pathway. The disciples walked proudly alongside Jesus. The crowd followed behind, singing praises. "Praise God, Hosanna," they sang.

Not all the people were filled with joy and thanksgiving. Some of them hated Jesus. They wanted Him arrested. The cheering noise of the people angered them.

"Make these crowds be still," the Pharisees commanded Jesus. "Tell them to be quiet."

"If they keep quiet," Jesus answered, "I tell you, the very stones of Jerusalem will shout."

This made the people sing louder and shout even more praises: "Hosanna! Hosanna! Blessed is the King."

PALM SUNDAY MUSIC

Make a fan or palm leaf for each child by folding green construction paper.

Teach the children new words to the familiar tune, "This Is the Way We Wash Our Clothes" (words below).

Form two lines, with children facing one another as if standing and waiting for a parade. Have them hold up their palm leaves or fans. As they sing the first stanza, the children should stretch their necks as if looking for Jesus to come down the road.

As they sing the second stanza of the song, they should wave the leaves up and down, and then lay them on the ground.

As they sing the third stanza, the children should cup their hands around their mouths and lift their chins upward.

Have them get down on their knees and make praying hands as they sing the last stanza.

This is the way we watch for Him, watch for Him, watch for Him.
This is the way we watch for Him on Palm Sunday morning.

This is the way we welcome Him, welcome Him, welcome Him.
This is the way we welcome Him on Palm Sunday morning.

This is the way we sing our praise, sing our praise, sing our praise.
This is the way we sing our praise on Palm Sunday morning.

This is the way we pray to Him, pray to Him, pray to Him.
This is the way we pray to Him on Palm Sunday morning.

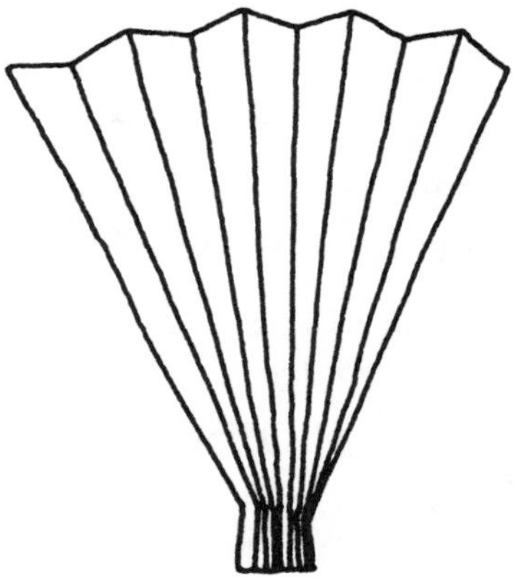

WINDOW ORNAMENT

Celebrate Palm Sunday by making a window ornament.

Materials:

Waxed paper
Construction paper
Tissue paper
Iron, on low setting
Crayon or marker
Glue
Pencil
Scissors

waxed paper

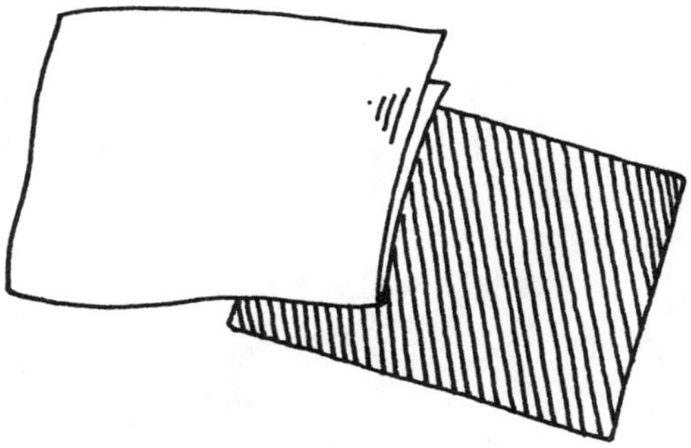

Directions:

Tear two pieces of waxed paper (about 8" long). Trace palm leaf below on green tissue paper and cut it out. Use brown tissue paper for the stem. Glue the palm leaf and stem on the center of one piece of waxed paper. Lay the other piece of waxed paper over the leaf and press it with a warm iron. (Adult help may be needed.) Cut a 7" x 7" square out of the center of a piece of construction paper. Place another sheet of construction paper under the cut one for the frame. Glue the waxed paper design between the two pieces of the frame. Trim away any extra waxed paper. Use a crayon or marker to write "Hosanna" on the frame.

Cut out

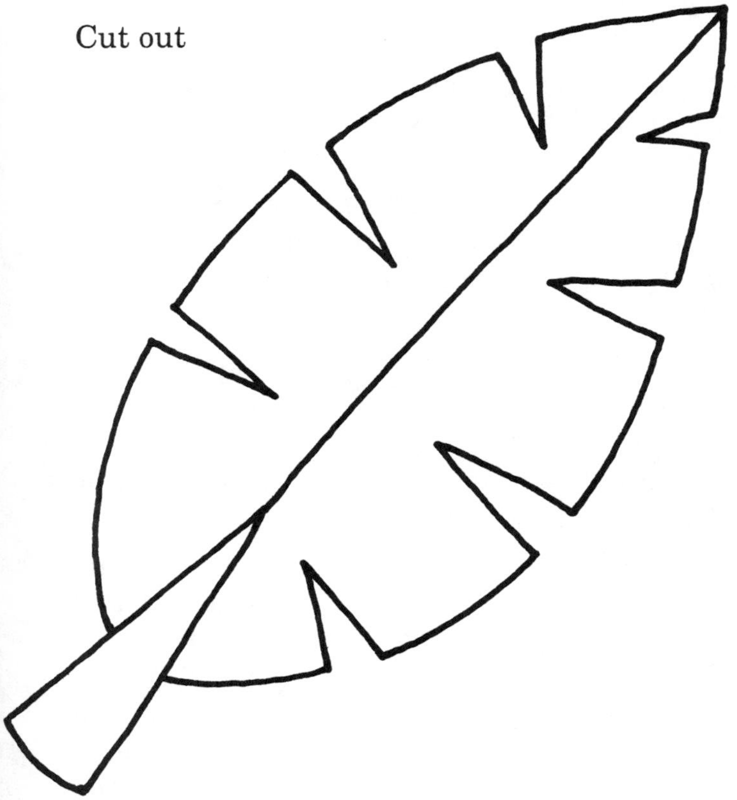

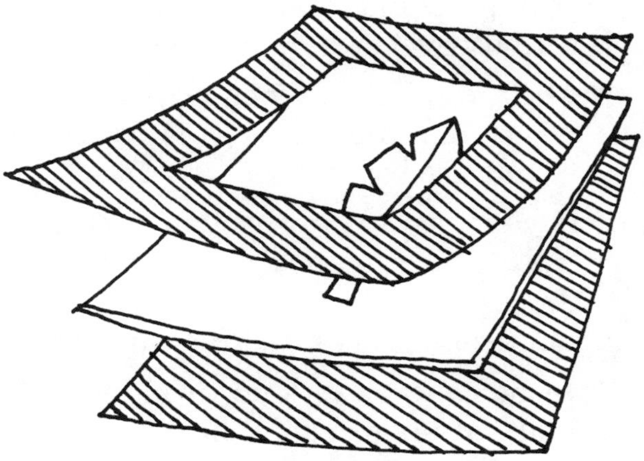

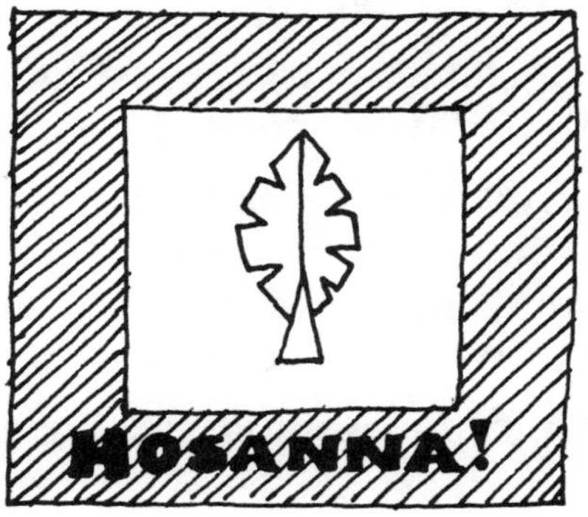
HOSANNA!

THE MARKET IN THE TEMPLE

Based on Matthew 21:12-17

Jesus had come to the temple in Jerusalem to teach people more about God's Law. As He walked into the courtyard, He heard arguing and yelling. Doves were squawking and sheep bleating. The temple didn't look like the house of the Lord at all. It looked like a marketplace.

Jesus stared in anger as He saw the money changers doing business and the bankers sitting behind tables, trading money so people could buy sacrifices. There was bustling activity everywhere, and noise, noise, noise!

All of a sudden a heavy table came crashing over. Cage doors flew open, and doves came flapping out. Coins rolled every which way. The moneylender screamed out, "What are you doing?"

It was Jesus. He threw over a table–crash! Then another table! More animals were freed, more money scattered. Jesus continued shoving tables and slinging money. Sheep were bleating, cows were lowing, birds were flying. Everywhere there was confusion, and Jesus was causing it.

Jesus' voice was loud and angry: "Listen, don't the Scriptures tell us what God has said? 'My house shall be called a house of prayer for all people.' You've turned it into a den of robbers! I am making it clean! Take all these things out!"

The Pharisees and scribes were furious with Jesus. They were determined to get rid of Him. "We must kill this man," they said, and they began to make their plans.

Crowds gathered around Jesus. He sat and waited for them to grow quiet. A blind man was led through the crowd. Jesus' face became gentle again. He lightly touched the man's eyes, and the man could see. The people cheered. Other sick people pushed and shoved their way toward Jesus so they, too, might be made well.

There were children standing nearby and they began shouting, "Hosanna to the Son of David!"

TEMPLE GAME

Flip a coin and move ahead one space for heads and two spaces for tails. Read each Bible verse on which you land. Play alone or with a friend.

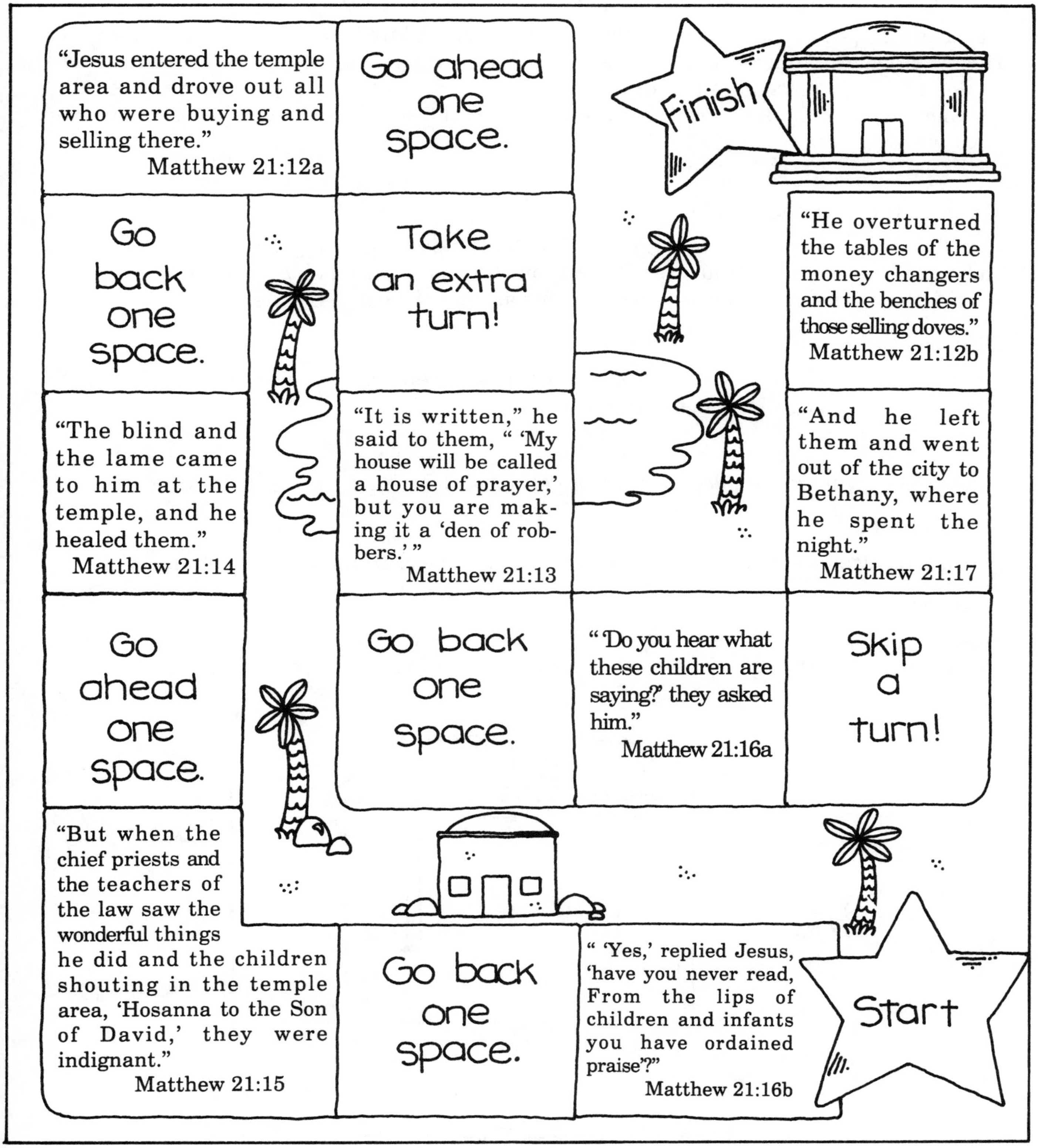
"Jesus entered the temple area and drove out all who were buying and selling there." Matthew 21:12a
Go ahead one space.
Finish
Go back one space.
Take an extra turn!
"He overturned the tables of the money changers and the benches of those selling doves." Matthew 21:12b
"The blind and the lame came to him at the temple, and he healed them." Matthew 21:14
"It is written," he said to them, " 'My house will be called a house of prayer,' but you are making it a 'den of robbers.' " Matthew 21:13
"And he left them and went out of the city to Bethany, where he spent the night." Matthew 21:17
Go ahead one space.
Go back one space.
"Do you hear what these children are saying?" they asked him." Matthew 21:16a
Skip a turn!
"But when the chief priests and the teachers of the law saw the wonderful things he did and the children shouting in the temple area, 'Hosanna to the Son of David,' they were indignant." Matthew 21:15
Go back one space.
" 'Yes,' replied Jesus, 'have you never read, From the lips of children and infants you have ordained praise'?" Matthew 21:16b
Start

A SPECIAL PLACE

Jesus was angry because many people did not respect the house of God. They did not use the temple for worship as they were supposed to. Jesus was also angry at the Pharisees because they did not want children to be there, singing praises to the Lord. The Lord wants all His people to praise Him and worship Him.

Set aside a special place in your classroom where children may worship the Lord. Let them help you plan how to make it special. What things will you need? (Ideas: A small table, a Bible, a piece of felt to drape across the table, a rug to lay in front of the table to kneel on.) Assemble these pieces and help children make some of those below for your worship area.

Candle and Candle Holder:

Form a piece of clay into a ball. Press a hole in the ball big enough to hold a candle. Put the candle in the hole and press clay around it so it stands by itself. Make a small wreath with pine branches or flowers to put around the candle holder.

Elegant Bookmark:

Knot together, at the top, four 12" pieces of different colored hair ribbon. Use each ribbon to mark a special page in the Bible.

Cross:

Find sticks or twigs outside. Tie them together with string for a rustic-looking cross.

Centerpiece:

Go on a nature hunt and find wildflowers, bark, leaves, etc. Arrange them in a vase.

Banner:

Design your pattern on a piece of paper. Transfer it to a large piece of felt. Glue a wooden dowel at the top of the banner as shown. Add yarn to hang it up.

Worship
the
Lord!

THE LAST SUPPER

Based on Matthew 26:17-30; Mark 14:12-26

Families and friends all over Jerusalem gathered to celebrate the Passover Feast. In each house people celebrated with roasted lamb, unleavened bread, side dishes, and bitter herbs.

While the rest of the city of Jerusalem was enjoying the celebration, Jesus sat with His twelve disciples in a quiet upper room. Jesus was at the head of the table. When the meal was about to begin, Jesus did not tell His disciples the Passover story as they had expected. Instead, Jesus began, "I tell you the truth, one of you is going to betray Me tonight."

The disciples were confused, "How could that be?" They loved Jesus. They would never betray Him. "Surely not I, Lord," each one said.

John asked, "Lord, who is it?"

Jesus answered, "It is the one to whom I will give this piece of bread when I have dipped it in the dish." Then He dipped the bread and handed it to Judas Iscariot.

"Surely not I, Teacher?" said the man who was about to betray His Lord for thirty silver coins.

"Yes," answered Jesus, "it is you. What you are about to do, go and do quickly." Judas left and went to talk to the Pharisees, to tell them where they could capture Jesus.

While they were eating, Jesus took some bread, blessed it, and began breaking it into pieces. Then He passed the broken bread to each of His disciples. He said, "Take and eat, for this is My body which is broken for you."

Then Jesus lifted the goblet of wine. After blessing it, He passed it to each of His disciples. "Take and drink. This wine is My blood which is shed for the forgiveness of sins."

This was a very important occasion that Jesus didn't want His disciples to ever forget. "As often as you eat this bread and drink this wine," He said, "remember Me."

After Jesus and His disciples sang a hymn, they left and went to the Mount of Olives to a garden to pray.

"REMINDERS OF GOD" QUILT

Make a class quilt with different colored pieces of construction paper as patches. Have students color pictures of things that remind them of God. Have them sign their "patches" and glue them several inches apart to a big piece of butcher paper. Draw small lines around each picture to look like thread marks.

Shelly
Mark
Debbie
Bible
John
Becky
Angie
Mindy
Bob
Ken

A SPECIAL "SUPPER"

Bring in some bread (pita bread or an uncut loaf) that may be torn into pieces and some grape juice. After washing their hands, have children sit around a table. Pass around the loaf of bread. Let each child tear off his own portion. Then hand out small paper cups of grape juice.

Remind the children that when the Jews celebrated the Last Supper, they "retold" the story of how God used Moses to lead His chosen people out of slavery in Egypt and into the Promised Land.

After eating the bread and drinking the juice, allow each child to "retell" a favorite Bible story.

BREAD DOUGH ORNAMENTS

Make bread dough ornaments as reminders of God's love.

Materials:

4 cups flour
$1^1/_2$ cups warm water
1 cup salt
Yarn

Mixing bowl
Baking sheet
Board
Knife

Plastic wrap
Foil
Acrylic paints
Paintbrushes

Salt

Directions:

1. Mix flour and salt in bowl.
2. Make a well in the center of the flour.
3. Pour in one cup of warm water, mixing with hands.
4. Add more water and continue mixing.
5. Knead for five minutes on a floured board until smooth. (At this point dough may be wrapped in plastic and put into refrigerator for later use.)
6. Roll out a small ball of dough on floured board or foil.
7. Use a dull knife to cut an ornament shape. Put a hole in the top so it can be hung later.
8. Bake at 325° one hour or until hard.
9. When ornament is cool, use paints to decorate it or write a message on it.
10. Hang with a piece of yarn.

He is King!
Jesus
Lord

THE CAPTURE OF JESUS

Based on Matthew 26:36-56; Mark 14:32-52; Luke 22:47-53; John 18:1-11

Jesus prayed in the Garden of Gethsemane. His heart was heavy on this night. He knew He would soon be suffering for the sins of the whole world. "Father, everything is possible for You. Take this cup from Me."

Jesus knew that God had the power to instantly take Him up to heaven with Him. There would be no pain or suffering there. But Jesus also knew why God had sent Him to earth. He knew He must suffer and die so that all men might be saved. Jesus ended His prayer by saying, "Do not do what I want, but what You want."

While Jesus prayed, the disciples slept nearby. Even though Jesus had asked them to keep watch, they could not stay awake even for one hour. Jesus walked over to where they were lying. "Are you still sleeping and resting?" He asked. "Enough! The hour has come. Let us go! Here comes My betrayer!"

As He was speaking, the lights of many torches came into view. Soldiers armed with swords and clubs pushed forward. Chief priests and Pharisees walked behind them.

Jesus asked them, "Who is it you want?"

"Jesus of Nazareth," they replied.

Judas, one of the disciples, was standing with the chief priests. He stepped forward and kissed Jesus on the cheek. This was the sign for the soldiers to know who they were to arrest. Judas had betrayed his teacher and master, an innocent man, for thirty silver coins.

Jesus looked into the eyes of Judas and said, "Do you betray Me with a kiss?"

With that, the soldiers stepped forward to arrest Jesus. Peter quickly took his sword and lashed out at one of the high priests, cutting off his ear.

"Put your sword back in its place," Jesus said to him. He touched the man's ear and healed him. "Don't you know that I could call on My Father and He would send thousands of angels to rescue Me?" Jesus said. He wanted His disciples to understand. "But God's Word says that it must happen this way. So let it be as He has said."

HEART TALK

Make a heart-shaped beanbag.

Materials:

Heavy cloth
Scissors
Sewing machine
Stuffing
Beans
Needle
Thread

Directions:

1. Using the pattern below, cut two pieces of heavy cloth in a heart shape.
2. Place the right sides of the material together. Use a sewing machine to stitch around the edges of the heart, leaving a small opening for stuffing.
3. Fill the heart with beans; then stitch the opening closed.

Have the children stand in a circle. Hold the heart and talk about something you would like to pray for or something heavy on your heart. When you are done, gently toss the beanbag to a child. It's his turn to share. (If the child doesn't wish to share, let him toss the heart to someone who has not yet shared.)

Remind children that when Jesus had something heavy on His heart, He talked to God about it. We can do the same.

PRAYER BANNER

glue

Materials:

Felt (blue, white, and black)
Glue
Yarn
Black marker
Pencil
Scissors
Hole punch

Directions:

1. Trim an 8" x 11" piece of blue felt in a banner shape.
2. Trace and cut out the figure of Jesus below on a white piece of felt. (Use black felt for His shadow.)
3. Glue the figures on the banner as shown.
4. Use a marker to write Jesus' words, "Not My will, but Yours be done" on the banner.
5. Punch holes at the top of the banner and tie with yarn for hanging.

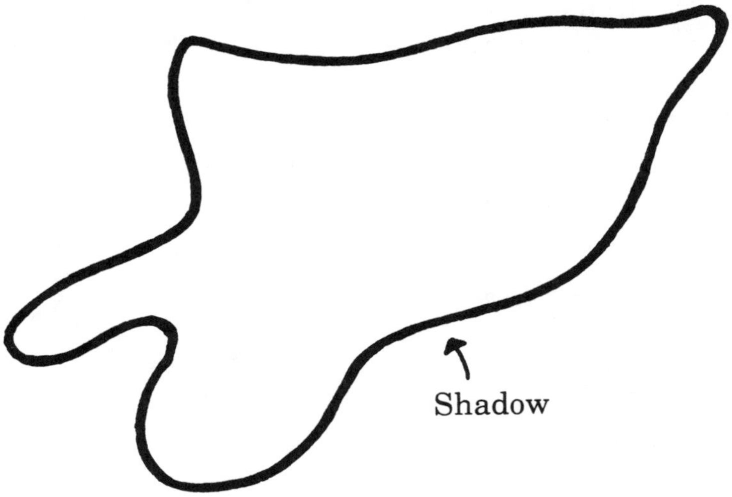

Shadow

Not My will,
but Yours be done.

JESUS BEFORE PILATE

Based on Mark 15:1-20; Luke 23:1-25; John 18:28-40; 19:1-16

Whips stung Jesus' skin. Blood and sweat dripped down His back. The soldiers pushed and shoved, laughing and making fun of Him.

"So, You are the King?" they sneered. "You don't look like a king. You have no robe, no crown." They spoke with hatred. The soldiers had taken Jesus' clothes. He was beaten and bruised, but Jesus stood silently before them.

The soldiers found a purple robe and laid it on Jesus' blistered back. A branch of thorns was twisted into a circle and pushed hard onto His head. Blood dripped down His face.

The soldiers continued to mock Him: "Hail, King of the Jews!" They spun Him around in circles, struck Him in the face, and spat on Him.

Then Jesus was sent to the governor, Pilate. Pilate didn't hate Jesus as the others did. He felt sorry for Him. He asked Him questions, hoping that Jesus would give the right answers so he could let Him go.

"Are You the King of the Jews?"

"Yes, I am," Jesus replied.

"Don't You hear how many things they are accusing You of?"

Jesus was silent.

Pilate could find no fault with Jesus and wanted to let Him go. Each year at Passover, it was the governor's custom to let one prisoner go free. Pilate thought this would be a good chance to release Jesus. So he asked the people if they wanted him to set Jesus free.

Another man named Barabbas was also a prisoner. The elders and chief priests wanted Jesus to die. They led the crowd by shouting, "Barabbas! We want you to set Barabbas free!" The people's voices joined in and grew louder.

Pilate was confused as he spoke to the crowd. "What shall I do then, with Jesus who is called Christ?"

They all answered, "Crucify Him!"

"But what has He done?" asked Pilate.

The crowd only shouted louder, "Crucify Him, crucify Him!"

When Pilate saw that the crowd would not change their minds, he knew what must be done. He called for a bowl of water; then washed his hands in front of the people. "I am innocent of this man's blood," he said. "It is your responsibility."

The people answered, "Let His blood be on us and on our children!"

Pilate released Barabbas and handed Jesus over to be crucified.

SPRING IN A BAG

1. Give each child a paper bag with his name on it. Take a spring walk to observe and collect some wonderful things God has made, such as grass, clover, wildflowers, leaves, twigs, and ladybugs.
2. While the children are collecting, have them take a deep breath, smell the different things they find, and close their eyes and touch the items.
3. Encourage the children to name all the different colors they see around them.
4. Seat children in a circle on the grass. Have them close their eyes and listen. What sounds do they hear that are God's sounds? People's sounds? Which are better?
5. Have the children lie down on their backs, look up at the sky, and watch the clouds move, noticing how they change shapes.
6. Talk about the air. Does it feel cold, hot, "tickley," dry, wet? Let children take off their shoes to feel the air with their feet.
7. Have each child crouch down and look around to see what the world is like to a little bug or animal.
8. Encourage the children to share their thoughts about the spring day and the wonderful world God has made.
9. The items that are placed in the bags may be taken back to the classroom and shared, then taken home.

CLOTHESPIN LAMB

Materials:

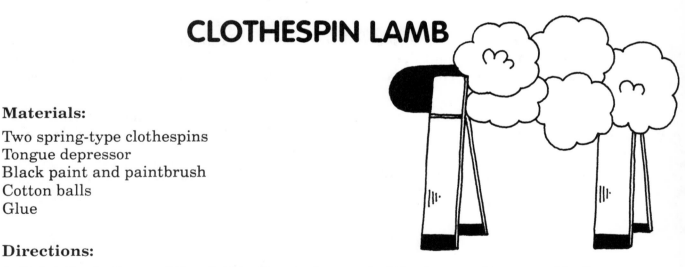

Two spring-type clothespins
Tongue depressor
Black paint and paintbrush
Cotton balls
Glue

Directions:

1. Paint the bottoms of the clothespins and an end of the tongue depressor black.
2. Place the tongue depressor between two clothespins to form the body of a lamb (with the black end of the tongue depressor sticking out).
3. Glue cotton balls to the body of the lamb. (Make sure to leave the black part of the tongue depressor showing for the lamb's face.)

Explain to children that Jesus was called the Lamb of God because He died like a sacrificial lamb for our sins.

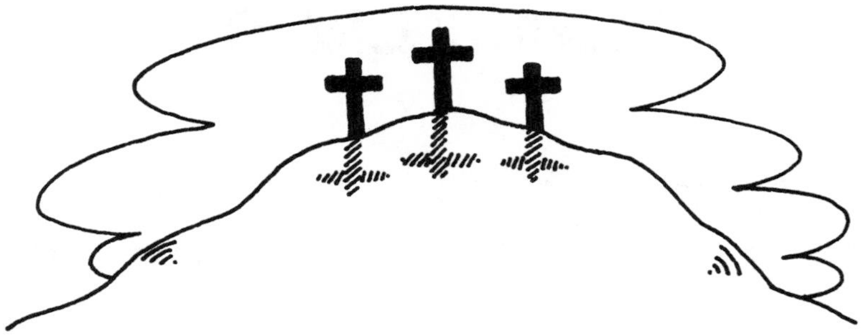

ON THE CROSS

Based on Matthew 27:32-55; Mark 15:21-40; Luke 23:26-49; John 19:17-30

The sun came up as usual. The sounds of a rooster crowing could be heard. Soldiers had whipped Jesus until late into the night. A tired, aching Jesus limped along the path, dragging a heavy wooden cross. He weaved back and forth until at last He fell near a man named Simon. The soldiers forced Simon to carry Jesus' cross. Many people followed behind as they made their way to a hill called the Skull.

Two other men, both criminals, were crucified next to Jesus–one on His right, the other on His left.

As Jesus hung on the cross, the rulers said, "He saved others; let Him save Himself if He is the Christ of God, the chosen one."

Jesus was not full of hatred for the people around Him. He felt pity. "Father," He said, "forgive them, for they do not know what they are doing."

Pilate had a sign placed above Jesus' head. It read, "This is the King of the Jews."

Some people made fun of Jesus while He hung on the cross in great pain. One of the robbers hanging next to Jesus shouted cruel remarks. The other robber spoke out, "We are getting what we deserve, but this man has done nothing wrong." He slowly turned his head to Jesus and said, "Remember me when You come into Your kingdom."

Jesus answered him, "Today you will be with Me in paradise."

Mary, Jesus' mother, stood weeping at the foot of the cross. What sadness she felt as she saw her son dying. Jesus' disciple John stood beside her.

When Jesus saw His mother and His disciple He said, "Dear woman, here is your son." Jesus said to John, "Here is your mother." From that time on, John took Mary into his home.

The hours passed as Jesus' pain continued to grow. At noon, darkness came upon the whole world for three hours. God's creation was mourning the death of His Son.

Jesus cried out in a loud voice, "My God, My God, why have You forsaken Me?" Then He whispered, "I am thirsty."

A soldier standing by fastened a sponge on a stick and soaked it in wine vinegar. He gave it to Jesus. After Jesus' lips had tasted the wine, He said, "It is finished. Father, into Your hands I commit My spirit." Then He died.

CALVARY CRAFTS

Decorative Cross:

1. Glue two craft sticks together to form a cross.
2. Using markers, stickers, glitter, macaroni, small buttons, or other pretty things, decorate the cross.
3. To make a hanger, glue a pop-top ring or a small loop of string on the back of the top of the cross.

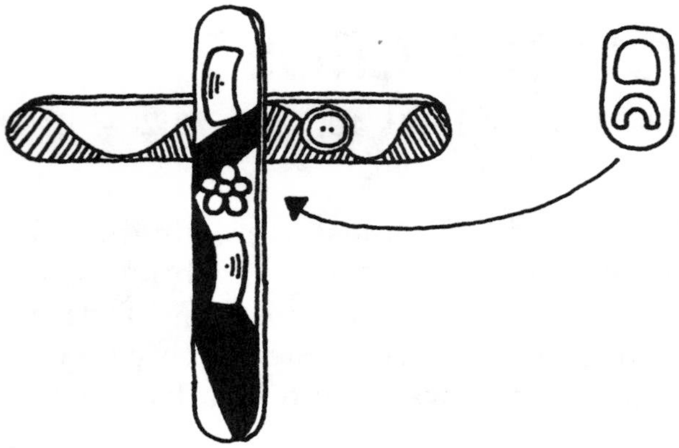

Cookie Treats:

Bake cross-shaped cutout cookies. Decorate them with icing and cookie sprinkles.

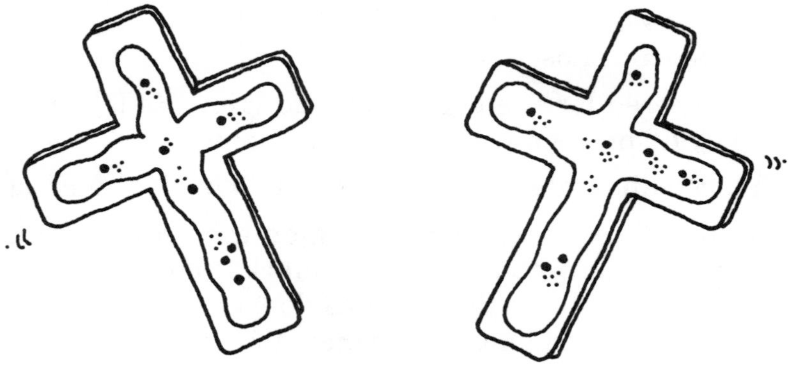

Sand Art:

Use a pencil to draw a picture of three crosses on a hill. Squirt white glue in thin lines over the pencil marks. Sprinkle plain or colored dry sand all over the paper. Let the glue dry until it feels hard when you touch it. Shake the loose sand off the paper.

Dyed Rice Mosaic:

1. Dye uncooked rice different colors. Place it in containers of water and pour food coloring over it. (The less water, the more intense the color.)
2. Spread the rice on a newspaper to dry, keeping the colors separate.
3. Draw a simple design on stiff paper or cardboard.
4. Working on one section of design at a time, spread glue so it covers the entire section.
5. Sprinkle colored rice on top of the glue. Repeat with each section of the design.
6. After the glue has dried, outline the design with yarn.

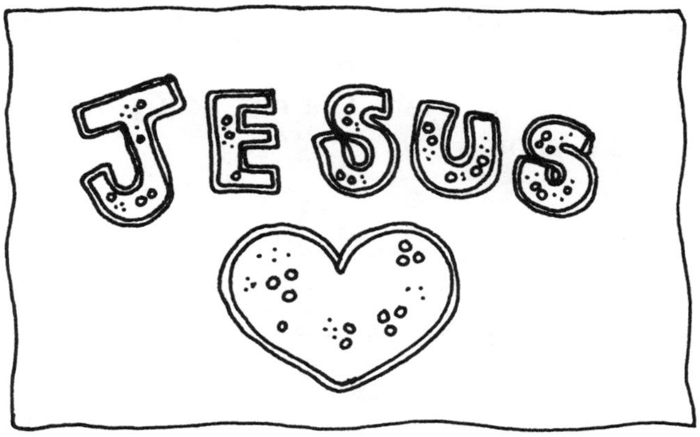
JESUS

New Life Collage:

Materials:
Magazines
Scissors
Construction paper
Glue

Directions:

Jesus rose from the dead and lives again. Think about the signs of new life all around each spring–flowers, butterflies, baby birds, and green leaves. Look through magazines and cut out pictures of new life we see each spring. Glue the pictures to a sheet of construction paper to form a collage. Take a nature walk and find seeds, leaves, or flower petals to include on your collage.

Calvary Crosses:

Materials:

Cigar box or candy box with hinged lid
Construction paper
Craft sticks
Dirt
Grass seed
Plastic wrap
Glue
Small cup of water

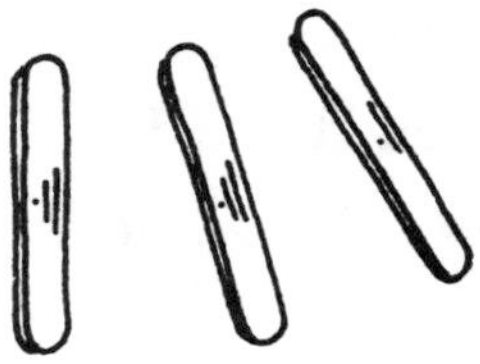

Directions:

Open the lid of the box and glue blue construction paper on the inside cover to represent the sky. Cut clouds and sun from construction paper and glue them on the sky. Line the bottom of the box with plastic wrap; then fill the box with dirt. Make three crosses from craft sticks. Stand the crosses in the dirt. Sprinkle with grass seed. Lightly sprinkle water on the seed. Place the box in a sunny place and keep the soil moist. In a few days the grass should begin to grow.

EASTER MORNING

Based on Matthew 27:57-66; 28:1-10; Mark 15:42-47; 16:1-8; Luke 23:50-56; 24:1-9

It was early morning. A dim outline of a large stone could be seen. It was rolled in front of a tomb. Soldiers marched back and forth, guarding the area.

The enemies of Jesus felt they had nothing to fear now. They had watched Jesus die slowly on a cross. They had seen His side pierced. They had watched His bruised body being wrapped in white linens and carried off to His tomb. By sealing the tomb with a large stone, they had seen to it that no man could enter and steal Jesus' body.

Yet, the enemies of God remembered the terrifying signs they had watched with their own eyes. The bright sun had blackened, and the earth had been shaken. They remembered that Jesus had said that after three days He would rise from the grave.

Suddenly the earth began to tremble. The guards jumped to their feet and drew their swords. A mighty angel of God appeared. He rolled back the stone from the tomb and sat on it. His face was like lightning and he looked as white as snow.

The guards were terrified. They fell to the ground and lay there as if they were dead.

Jesus had risen from the dead!

Sounds of women coming down the path could be heard. They were walking slowly with their heads bent in grief. They were faithful friends of Jesus who had come carrying perfumes to put on His body.

"Who shall roll away the stone from the door of the tomb?" they asked. The stone was much too heavy for them to move. But when they reached the tomb, they saw that the great stone had already been rolled away. The guards were no longer there.

The women were confused and afraid. They slowly peeked through the opening and edged their way into the opened tomb. Jesus' body was not there.

The women looked up and saw two men that shone like lightning. Terrified, the women bowed down.

The angels spoke to them. "What are you doing here? Jesus is not here. He has risen!"

Joyfully, the women ran to tell the others, "Jesus is alive! Jesus is alive!"

EASTER FRIEZE

colored
pencils

Materials:

Construction paper
Long strip of paper
Glue
Scissors
Crayons or colored pencils

Directions:

1. Cut a piece of drawing paper 4 $^{1}/_{2}$" x 14".
2. Fold the paper in half; then fold it again as shown.

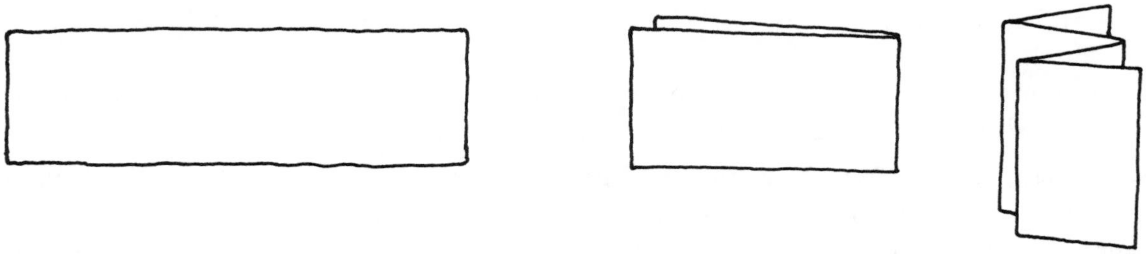

3. Cut a sheet of construction paper 9" x 5" and fold in half for a cover.
4. Glue the first folded section to the inside of the cover as shown.
5. Copy and color the pictures of Easter week on pages 81 and 82.
6. Cut out the pictures and glue them in the book in the proper order.
7. Decorate the front cover.
8. Using your frieze, retell the story of Palm Sunday through Easter.

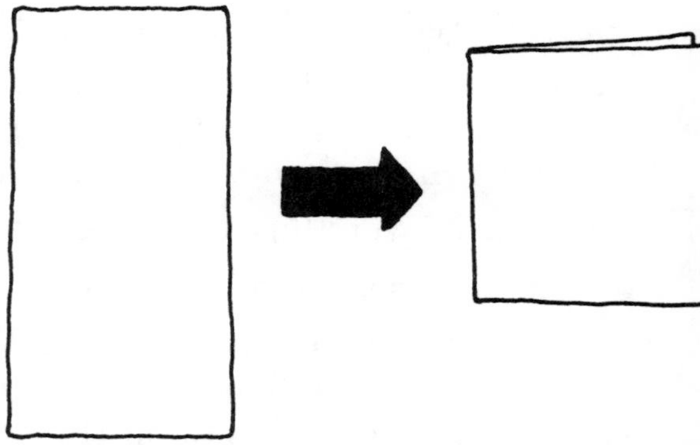

4
5
6
7

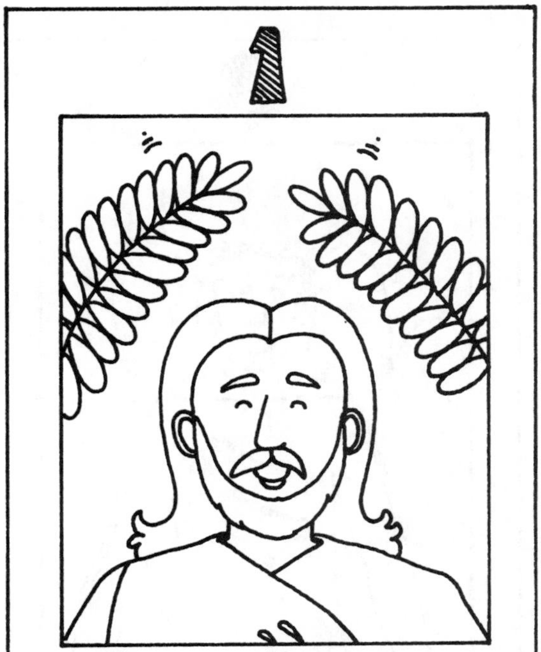

Palm Sunday

Jesus in the Temple

The Last Supper

4

Jesus Praying in Gethsemane

5

Jesus Before Pilate

6

Jesus Dies on the Cross

7

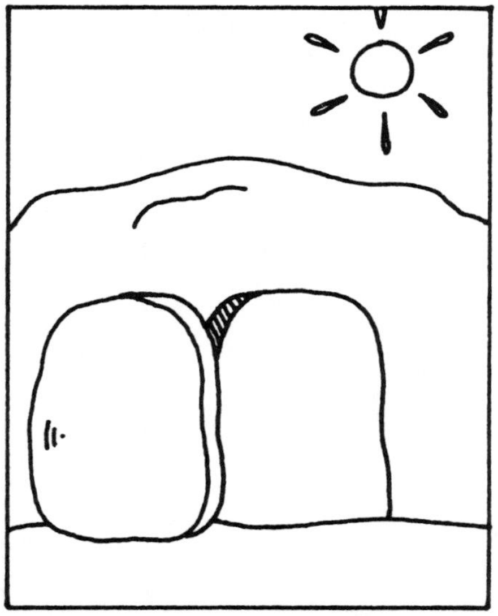

Jesus Rises from the Dead

DOUBTING THOMAS

Based on John 20:19-31

Jesus appeared to a group of His disciples on the evening of His resurrection. He showed them the marks on His hands and feet, where the nails had pierced Him. He let the disciples touch Him to convince themselves that He had flesh and bones. Jesus ate with them to prove that it was He and no one else. What joy the disciples felt! Jesus had truly risen from the grave!

He sat with His beloved disciples and said to them, "As My Father sent Me, even so I send you."

Thomas, one of Jesus' disciples, was not with the others when Jesus appeared, so the disciples were anxious to share the wondrous news about their Lord and Savior. They explained to Thomas how Jesus had come to them. Yes, He had truly risen from the grave.

As the disciples breathlessly shared the news, Thomas shook his head in disbelief. "It's just not possible," said the doubting disciple. "Unless I see the nail marks in His hands and put my finger where the nails were, and put my hand into His side, I will not believe it." The disciples continued trying to convince Thomas of the Lord's resurrection, but he only shook his head.

A week later the disciples were in the house again. This time, Thomas was with them. Though the doors were locked, Jesus came and stood among them saying, "Peace be with you!" Then He said to Thomas, "Put your finger here where the nails were, and put your hand into My side. Stop doubting and believe."

Thomas was amazed that the Lord used his exact words. This truly was the Son of God! Thomas threw himself down at Jesus' feet and cried out, "My Lord and my God!"

Jesus said to Thomas, "Because you have seen Me, you have believed; blessed are those who have not seen and yet have believed."

Jesus knew that in the years to come many others would learn about Him. They would not touch His wounds or see the scars in His skin. Yet, they would believe that Jesus rose so that all men might be free and that Jesus was truly the Son of God.

DISCIPLE MEMORY GAME

Use eleven paper plates to represent the disciples that saw Jesus after He had risen. Write a disciple's name on each of the plates. Hand out the plates and have each child draw a face for a disciple.

Write the children's names on a sheet of paper or the chalkboard to record their success. Put the plates on the floor. Pass out eleven fish crackers for each player. Take turns tossing crackers onto each of the plates. When a cracker lands on a plate, the player calls out the name of that disciple. The player with the most crackers (recorded marks) on the eleven plates is declared the winner.

Peter
Andrew
Bartholomew
James 1
James 2
Philip
John
Thaddaeus
Simon
Thomas
Matthew

"JESUS" BOOKMARK

glue

Materials:

Hole punch
Construction paper
Glue
Scissors
Poster board
Yarn

Directions:

Copy and cut out the bookmark pattern below. Glue it on poster board. Use a hole punch to punch "dots" from different colors of construction paper. Glue the dots on the letters. Punch a hole in the top and tie a piece of yarn for the tassel.

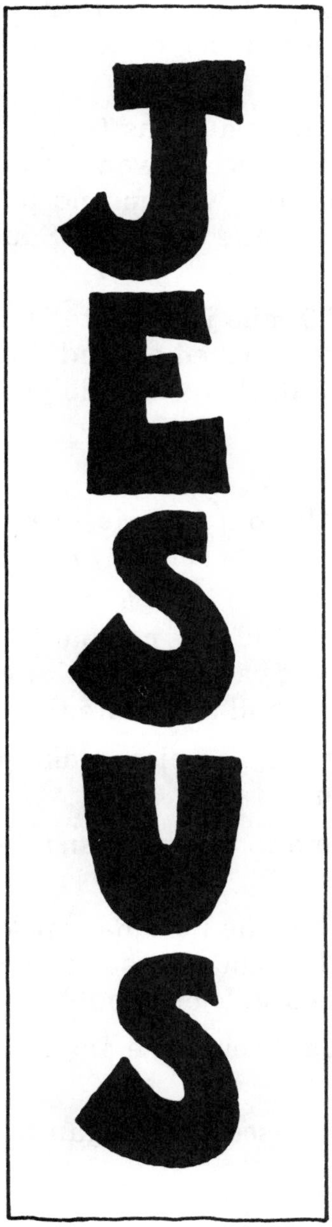
JESUS

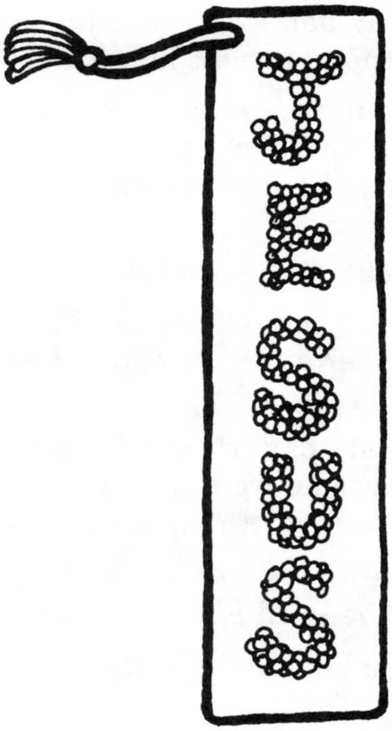
JESUS

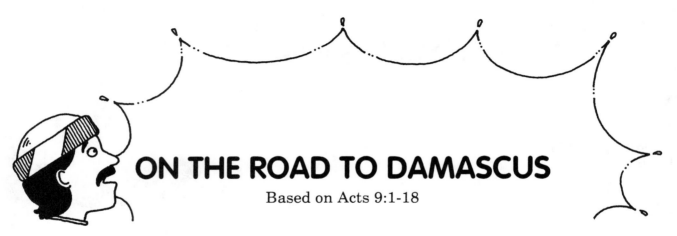

ON THE ROAD TO DAMASCUS

Based on Acts 9:1-18

After Jesus rose from the dead, He stayed on earth for forty days. During that time, He appeared often to His disciples and spoke to them about the kingdom of God. He gave them power to heal the blind and the sick and to perform other miracles in His name.

After Jesus went back to heaven, Christian groups began to form. The members listened as the disciples preached God's Word. The number of believers continued to grow.

Not everyone who heard the disciples believed that Jesus was God's Son. One such person was Saul. He spoke out loudly against Christians. He went through the city of Jerusalem, from house to house, dragging off men and women and putting them in prison. Many believers went to other places in Judea and Samaria. Saul continued to search for them, to rid the world of Jesus' followers.

One day Saul and some companions set off on a 150-mile journey to Damascus. When the trip was nearly over, a blinding light from heaven flashed around them. Saul fell to his knees on the ground. He heard a voice say, "Saul, Saul, why do you fight against Me?"

Saul cried out, "Who are you?"

"I am Jesus," said the voice. "You are arresting Me, putting Me in prison, yes, and killing Me over and over again. Get up and go into the city. There you will be told what you must do."

As Saul stood up, darkness fell around him. He was blind. His companions led him into the city, where he waited in a home for three days, not eating or drinking anything. He sat alone and sadly thought about all the believers he had mistreated.

He heard a knock at the door. "Brother Saul," a man's voice spoke gently. It was Ananias. "The Lord Himself has sent me to help you."

Saul was shaking as he asked, "Does God care for me so much? Aren't you afraid to be here with me?"

Ananias explained that at first he had been afraid, but the Lord had spoken to him and told him to come and lay his hands on Saul. "God has chosen you to do special work," explained Ananias. "You will preach His Word to the people of Israel."

Ananias laid his hands on Saul and immediately Saul could see again. He got up and was baptized.

For several days Saul talked to the believers in Damascus. He began to preach to the Jews, carrying the message of Jesus.

"SPREADING THE WORD" CRAFTS

Paul spread God's Word to many people while he lived. God wants us to spread His Word also. Here are several ways to practice telling your friends about Jesus.

Sock Puppets:

Draw faces on socks to make sock puppets. Let children team up and practice telling others about Jesus, using their puppets to talk to their friends' puppets.

Tin Can Telephone:

Make telephones to spread the "Good News." Poke a hole in the bottom of a tin can, then in another one. Knot string inside one can; then connect the string to the other can and knot it inside. Have children talk to one another through the cans.

Pass It:

Seat the children in a circle. Have a child whisper a Bible verse or message about Jesus to the person on his right, who then whispers the message he thinks he heard to the person on his right. Continue until the message reaches the last person in the circle, who tells the message out loud.

Pass it!

Friendly Letters:

Saul, who was later called Paul, was an Apostle of the Lord. After he met Jesus, he spent the rest of his life serving God. He wrote many letters to Christian congregations, encouraging the members to follow God's Law and to love one another. Those letters are books in the Bible. We can write letters to our friends to tell them about Jesus' love for them, much like Paul did.

Make personalized stationery using children's drawings, stamps, and stickers. Have the children write letters to their friends telling them that Jesus loves them. (See the felt printing ideas on the next page for decorating stationery.)

Felt Printing:

Materials:

Felt
Scissors
2" x 4" wood blocks or stiff cardboard
White glue
Shallow pan
Tempera paint
Newsprint
Plain paper
Envelopes

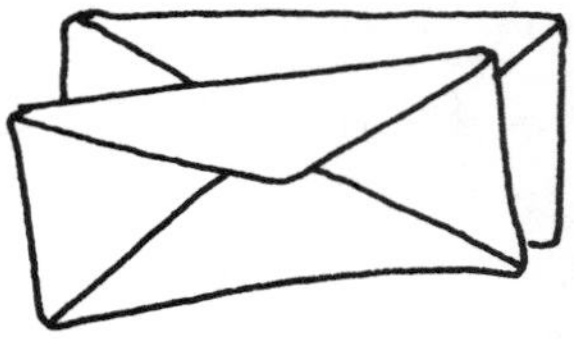

Directions:

1. Cut a felt piece into the shape desired.
2. Glue the shape on a wood block or stiff cardboard to make a stamp. Allow it to dry.
3. Dip the stamp into a shallow pan of tempera paint.
4. Press the stamp on newsprint to test it. When you're satisfied, use the stamp to decorate plain paper and envelopes.

1
2
3

4

CONCENTRATION

Reinforce Old Testament Bible stories by playing this matching game.

After copying the page, glue it to construction paper or poster board. Cut out the squares and place them facedown on a table. Let children take turns trying to match the pairs. (The Old Testament cards may be used as "wild" cards.)

Adam
Eve
Cain
Abel
Noah
Ark
David
Goliath
Daniel
Lion
Jonah
Big Fish
Shadrach, Meshach, Abednego
Fiery Furnace
Samson
Delilah
Moses
Pharaoh
Old Testament Story
Old Testament Story

QUESTION-AND-ANSWER MINI BOOK

Copy pages 91 and 92. Fold page 91 in half, then in half again to form a book. Unfold it and cut on the solid lines. Fold on the broken lines. Fold page 92 in half, then in half again. Unfold. Place page 91 on top of page 92 and refold to make question-and-answer mini book. Decorate the book with your own art work.

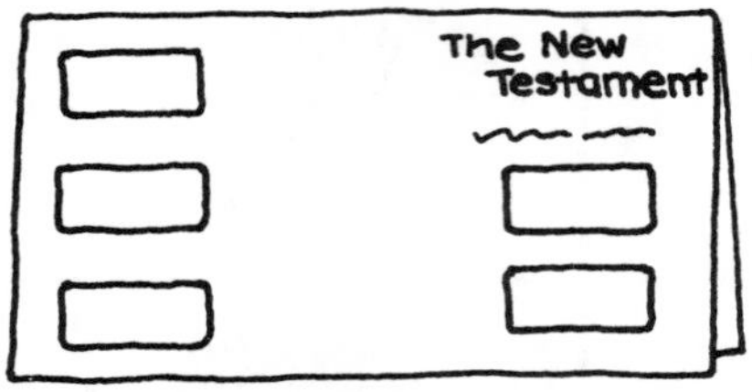

The New
Testament

1. Fold page 91 in half . . .

The New
Testament

2. and in half again.

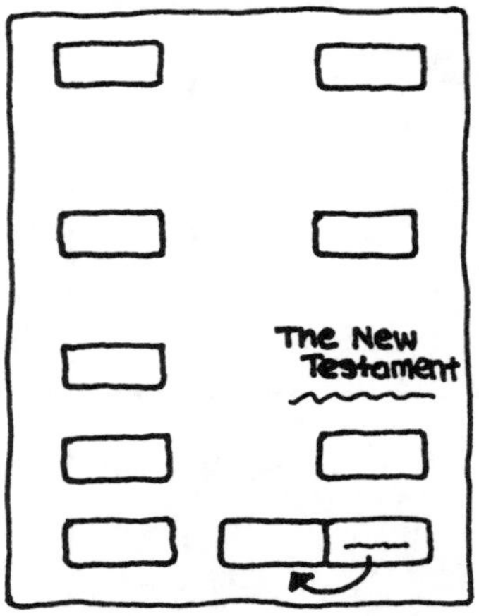

The New
Testament

3. Unfold and cut windows open.

The New
Testament
91

4. Place page 92 behind page 91.

The New
Testament
John the Baptist

5. Refold (as shown in steps 1 and 2) to make your mini book.

Where was
Jesus born?

Who is the Lamb of
God who takes away
the sin of the world?

Why did Jesus die
on the cross?

When Peter was
fishing, Jesus said to
him, "I will make you
fish for ______."

What were Jesus'
helpers called?

THE NEW TESTAMENT

Question-and-Answer Mini Book

What did Jesus give
the disciples to
remind them of His
body and blood?

Who baptized Jesus?

What disciple doubted
that Jesus rose from
the dead?

Who wrote many
letters to Christian
congregations?

In a stable in
Bethlehem

Jesus

To save us from
our sins

men

Disciples

Bread and
Wine

John the Baptist

Doubting
Thomas

Paul

BIBLE REVIEW
TWO-MINUTE FUN FILLERS

Who Am I?

Pretend to be a character in the Bible. Talk about how you feel. Talk about the members of your family. Say the prayers you might pray. Let the children guess who you are.

Story Stopper

Begin telling a Bible story. Stop in the middle of a sentence and let a child take it from there. Have the child continue until you say stop. Then another child may take up the story.

Twenty Questions

Think of a Bible story. Let the children ask twenty questions to help them guess the story. The questions may be answered only with yes or no.

Alphabet Fun

Call out a letter of the alphabet. Have the children suggest people in the Bible whose names begin with that letter.

Call out a letter of the alphabet. Have the children name books in the Bible that begin with that letter.

One-Word Clue

Have a child think of a story in the Bible. Let him give a one-word clue to help the other children guess the story. (Examples: Lion–Daniel in the lions' den; Ark–Noah's ark)

Create a Bible Story

Use story starters to help the children tell their own creative Bible stories. (Example: "One day I was walking along a dirt path on my way to Egypt, and you'll never guess who I saw . . . .")

Knowing Numbers

Call out a number. See who can name a Bible story with that number in it. (Examples: 1–One true God; 2–Two animals of each kind on the ark; 3–Jesus rose in three days)

A
Adam starts with A...
So does Abel!

Jump Rope Jingles

Jump for joy for Jesus.
Praise, praise His name.
Sing Alleluia.
Thank God He came.

God made the mountains.
God made the sea.
Name things God made
That start with letter A . . . B . . . C . . . D . . . .

Adam in the garden.
Zacchaeus in the tree.
How many names,
Can you say from A to Z?

Books in the Bible,
Sixty-six in all.
How many can you name
Before you trip and fall?

Animals in the ark,
Not all the same.
How many animals
Can you name?

66

CHARADES

For a review, act out Bible stories in a game of charades. Let a child draw a slip of paper that has the name of a Bible story written on it. (You may prefer to whisper the name of the story to the child if he can't read.) The child should act out the story while the rest of the children guess what it is. (The child may choose a helper if necessary.)

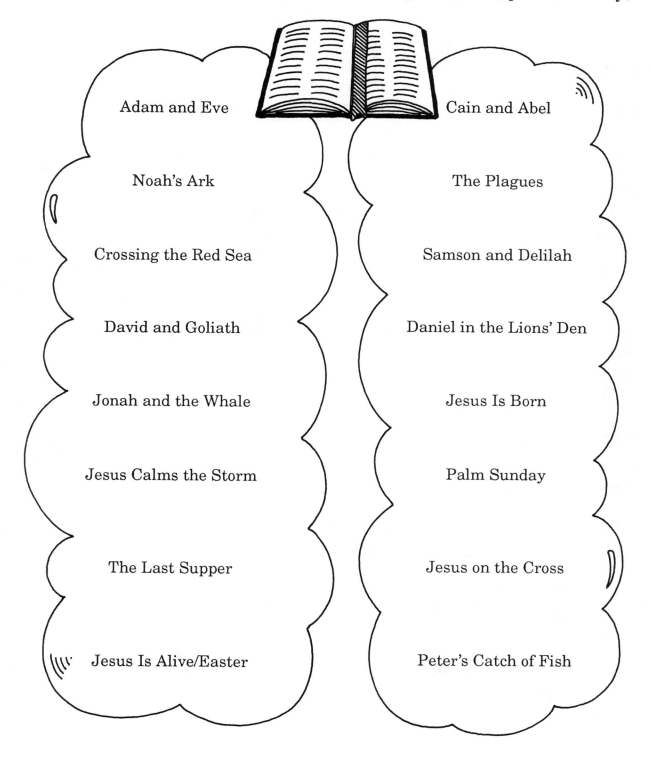

- Adam and Eve
- Noah's Ark
- Crossing the Red Sea
- David and Goliath
- Jonah and the Whale
- Jesus Calms the Storm
- The Last Supper
- Jesus Is Alive/Easter
- Cain and Abel
- The Plagues
- Samson and Delilah
- Daniel in the Lions' Den
- Jesus Is Born
- Palm Sunday
- Jesus on the Cross
- Peter's Catch of Fish

Sunshine Award

____
(name)

You bring sunshine to my life.

"Those who are wise will
shine like the brightness of
the heavens . . . ."
Daniel 12:3

______________________ ______________________
(teacher) (date)